THE CHEMISTRY OF LOVE

The Science Behind Love, Sex, and Attraction

Dr. Maxwell Shimba

Printed in the United States of America

SHIMBA
PUBLISHING

TABLE OF CONTENTS

INTRODUCTION

Welcome to "The Chemistry Between Us," a journey into the fascinating world of romantic attraction and relationships. As we delve into the complexities of love, we will explore how biological, psychological, and social factors intertwine to create the profound connections that define our romantic lives. This book aims to provide a comprehensive understanding of the science behind attraction and offer practical insights to help individuals and couples navigate the intricate dynamics of their relationships.

Romantic attraction is a universal experience that has intrigued humans for centuries. From poets and philosophers to scientists and psychologists, the quest to understand the nature of love has spanned diverse fields and perspectives. In this book, we will draw on an interdisciplinary approach, integrating knowledge from biology, psychology, sociology, and technology to paint a holistic picture of how attraction works. This integration will allow us to appreciate the multi-dimensional nature of love and uncover the myriad factors that influence our romantic choices and behaviors.

At the core of romantic attraction lies a complex interplay of biological mechanisms. We will begin our exploration by examining the role of neurotransmitters and hormones in shaping our feelings of love and attachment. The rush of dopamine during the early stages of infatuation, the calming effects of serotonin, and the bonding power of oxytocin all contribute to the intense emotions associated with romantic love. Understanding these chemical processes provides a foundation for appreciating how our bodies and brains are wired for connection.

Beyond biology, psychological factors play a crucial role in determining how we experience attraction and form relationships. Attachment theory, for instance, offers valuable insights into how early childhood experiences with caregivers shape our adult romantic relationships. By exploring different attachment styles, we can better understand our own relationship patterns and learn how to cultivate healthier, more secure connections. Additionally, cognitive biases and emotional intelligence are key components that influence how we perceive and interact with potential partners.

The social and cultural context in which we live also significantly impacts our romantic lives. Societal norms, cultural values, and evolving gender roles shape what we find attractive and how we approach relationships. Media and popular culture, with their depictions of love and beauty, further influence our perceptions and expectations. By examining these external factors, we can gain a deeper understanding of how our environment molds our romantic experiences and learn to navigate these influences more consciously.

Technological advancements have revolutionized the way we form and maintain romantic relationships. The rise of online dating platforms, social media, and virtual reality offers new opportunities and challenges for modern love. We will explore how these technologies affect our romantic interactions, from the initial spark of attraction to the maintenance of long-term relationships. By understanding the benefits and pitfalls of digital romance, we can harness technology to enhance our connections while avoiding potential drawbacks.

Finally, we will address some of the common challenges that can disrupt romantic relationships, such as stress, socioeconomic factors, and infidelity. By offering practical strategies for managing these issues, this book aims to equip readers with the tools they need to build resilient and fulfilling relationships. Communication, trust-building, and emotional support are crucial elements that will be emphasized throughout our discussion.

"The Chemistry Between Us" is not just a scientific exploration; it is also a guide for personal growth and relationship enhancement. Whether you are single and seeking to understand your romantic preferences, in a relationship and looking to deepen your connection, or simply curious about the science of love, this book has something to offer. By the end of our journey, you will have gained a richer understanding of the forces that drive attraction and the skills to foster healthier, more satisfying relationships.

Join me as we embark on this exploration of the chemistry of attraction. Together, we will uncover the secrets of love and learn how to cultivate the meaningful connections that bring joy and fulfillment to our lives.

x

DR. MAXWELL SHIMBA

UNDERSTANDING THE COMPLEX INTERPLAY OF BIOLOGY, PSYCHOLOGY, AND SOCIOLOGY IN ATTRACTION

Attraction is a multifaceted phenomenon that has intrigued humanity for centuries. Its complexity arises from the intricate interplay of biological, psychological, and sociological factors. Each domain offers unique insights into why we are drawn to certain individuals and how these attractions shape our relationships and social structures.

The Biological Foundations of Attraction

Biology provides the foundational layer of attraction, rooted in our evolutionary history. The drive to attract and be attracted is fundamental to the survival of our species. This drive is influenced by a variety of factors, including genetics, hormones, and neurotransmitters.

Genetics and Attraction:

Genetic compatibility plays a crucial role in attraction. Research suggests that we are often subconsciously attracted to individuals with different immune system genes (Major Histocompatibility Complex - MHC) than our own. This diversity enhances the immune system strength of potential offspring, promoting survival.

Hormones and Neurotransmitters:

Hormones like testosterone and estrogen significantly influence sexual attraction. Testosterone is linked to increased libido and assertiveness, while estrogen enhances nurturing behaviors and emotional bonding. Neurotransmitters such as dopamine, serotonin, and oxytocin are critical in the brain's reward and pleasure systems, reinforcing behaviors that lead to attraction and attachment. Dopamine, often called the "feel-good" neurotransmitter, spikes during the early stages of attraction, creating feelings of euphoria and excitement. Oxytocin, known as the "love hormone," is released during physical intimacy and helps cement long-term bonds.

Psychological Perspectives on Attraction

Psychology delves into the mental and emotional processes underlying attraction. This domain examines how our thoughts, feelings, and past experiences shape whom we find attractive and why.

Attachment Theory:

Developed by John Bowlby, attachment theory posits that early relationships with caregivers form the blueprint for future romantic relationships. Secure attachment styles lead to healthy, stable relationships, while anxious or avoidant attachment styles can result in challenging romantic dynamics.

Cognitive and Emotional Factors:

Attraction is also influenced by cognitive processes, such as the perception of similarity, reciprocity, and physical attractiveness. We are often drawn to people who share our interests, values, and personality traits, as these similarities reduce uncertainty and increase the likelihood of a harmonious relationship. The reciprocity principle suggests that we are attracted to those who show an interest in us, reinforcing our self-esteem and sense of worth.

Sociological Influences on Attraction

Sociology explores how attraction is shaped by societal norms, cultural practices, and social structures. It emphasizes the role of social context in determining whom we find attractive and how we express our attraction.

Cultural Norms and Values:

Cultural norms dictate what is considered attractive in different societies. These norms can vary widely; for example, while some cultures value slimness, others may prize fuller figures. Cultural values also influence the traits we seek in partners, such as intelligence, kindness, or economic stability.

Social Exchange Theory:

This theory suggests that attraction is based on a cost-benefit analysis. We are drawn to individuals who offer the greatest rewards (e.g., companionship, love, support) with the least costs (e.g., conflict, effort). This pragmatic approach highlights how social and economic factors can influence romantic choices.

Media and Socialization:

Media plays a powerful role in shaping perceptions of attractiveness. Television, movies, and social media often present idealized images of beauty and romance, setting standards that influence personal preferences. Socialization processes, including family upbringing and peer interactions, further reinforce these media-driven ideals.

The Interconnectedness of Biological, Psychological, and Sociological Factors

While each domain offers valuable insights, it is the intersection of biology, psychology, and sociology that provides a comprehensive understanding of attraction. Biological impulses may initiate attraction, but psychological and sociological factors shape its development and expression.

For instance, an individual's biological predisposition towards a high libido (biological) might be expressed through their attachment style (psychological) and influenced by societal norms around dating and relationships (sociological). This interplay creates a dynamic and ever-evolving process, reflecting the complexity of human attraction.

The Evolutionary Perspective

Evolutionary psychology offers a unifying framework for understanding attraction. It posits that many of our attraction behaviors have evolved to enhance reproductive success. Traits that were advantageous for survival and reproduction became preferred, leading to the development of common patterns in human attraction.

Mate Selection and Reproductive Strategies:

Men and women have evolved different strategies for selecting mates based on reproductive roles. Men, who can father numerous offspring, tend to prioritize physical attractiveness and youth, indicators of fertility. Women, with a more significant investment in pregnancy and child-rearing, often prioritize resources and stability in a partner.

Sexual Selection:

Sexual selection, a concept introduced by Charles Darwin, explains how certain traits become attractive because they enhance an individual's reproductive success. Traits like physical strength, symmetry, and even specific behaviors can be indicators of good genes and overall fitness.

Conclusion

Attraction is a rich tapestry woven from the threads of biology, psychology, and sociology. Understanding its complexity requires appreciating the contributions of each domain and recognizing their interconnections. As we delve deeper into the science of attraction, we uncover the profound ways in which our bodies, minds, and societies influence whom we love and why. This knowledge not only satisfies our curiosity but also enriches our relationships, helping us navigate the intricate dance of attraction with greater awareness and empathy.

HISTORICAL PERSPECTIVE ON THE STUDY OF HUMAN ATTRACTION

The Ancient World: Mythology and Philosophy

The study of human attraction has deep roots in ancient civilizations, where mythology and philosophy provided early frameworks for understanding the mysterious forces that draw people together. In Ancient Greece, for instance, the gods and goddesses of love—Aphrodite and Eros—symbolized the power and unpredictability of romantic attraction. The Greeks sought to explain human behavior through these deities, attributing passionate love and desire to divine influence.

Philosophers like Plato and Aristotle also offered early theories of attraction. Plato's concept of "platonic love" emphasized a deep, spiritual connection that transcended physical desire, while in his work "Symposium," he explored different kinds of love through a series of dialogues. Aristotle, on the other hand, approached attraction from a more practical perspective, considering the roles of friendship, mutual respect, and virtue in forming and sustaining relationships.

The Middle Ages: Courtly Love and Religious Influences

During the Middle Ages, the concept of courtly love emerged, heavily influenced by the social and religious contexts of the time. Courtly love was an idealized and often extramarital form of affection characterized by chivalry and admiration from afar. Troubadours and poets immortalized these romantic ideals in their works, celebrating the noble pursuit of love that transcended mere physical attraction.

Religious doctrines also played a significant role in shaping views on attraction. The Christian church promoted the sanctity of marriage and the virtue of chastity, emphasizing spiritual love over carnal desire. This period saw a dichotomy between the sacred and the secular, where love was either elevated to a divine plane or seen as a potential source of sin.

The Renaissance and Enlightenment: Science and Reason

The Renaissance marked a renewed interest in humanism and the natural world, leading to more scientific inquiries into human behavior, including attraction. Thinkers like Leonardo da Vinci and Michel de Montaigne began to explore the psychological and physiological aspects of love. This era laid the groundwork for later scientific studies by emphasizing observation and empirical evidence.

During the Enlightenment, the rise of rationalism further influenced the study of attraction. Philosophers such as John Locke and David Hume examined the role of reason and emotion in human relationships. Locke's theory of tabula rasa suggested that individuals are shaped by their experiences, including those related to attraction and love. Hume, meanwhile, emphasized the importance of passion and sentiment, arguing that reason alone could not account for the complexities of human affection.

The 19th Century: The Birth of Modern Psychology

The 19th century witnessed the birth of modern psychology, significantly advancing the study of human attraction. Sigmund Freud, often considered the father of psychoanalysis, introduced groundbreaking theories about the unconscious mind and the role of childhood experiences in shaping adult relationships. Freud's concepts of the Oedipus complex and libido highlighted the deep-seated psychological forces driving attraction and love.

William James, another pioneering psychologist, explored the interplay between emotion and cognition in his work "The Principles of Psychology." James proposed that emotions, including those related to attraction, were bodily responses to external stimuli, challenging earlier notions that emotions were purely mental states.

The 20th Century: Biological and Sociocultural Perspectives

The 20th century brought significant advancements in the scientific study of attraction, with researchers from various disciplines contributing to a more comprehensive understanding of the phenomenon. The rise of behavioral psychology, spearheaded by figures like B.F. Skinner and John Watson emphasized the role of environmental factors and learned behaviors in shaping attraction.

At the same time, advances in biology and genetics provided new insights into the physiological and evolutionary underpinnings of attraction. Researchers like Konrad Lorenz and Nikolaas Tinbergen studied animal behavior to draw parallels with human attraction, while sociobiologists such as Edward O. Wilson explored the genetic and evolutionary bases of social behaviors, including mate selection.

The Late 20th and Early 21st Century: Interdisciplinary Approaches

In recent decades, the study of attraction has become increasingly interdisciplinary, integrating insights from psychology, biology, sociology, and neuroscience. The advent of neuroimaging technologies, such as fMRI and PET scans, has allowed scientists to observe brain activity in real-time, providing a deeper understanding of the neural mechanisms underlying attraction.

Evolutionary psychology, popularized by researchers like David Buss and Steven Pinker, has continued to explore how evolutionary pressures shape human mating behaviors. This field emphasizes the adaptive functions of attraction, suggesting that many of our romantic preferences and behaviors are rooted in the need to maximize reproductive success.

Social psychology has also made significant contributions, with studies on attachment theory, interpersonal attraction, and the role of social and cultural factors in shaping romantic relationships. Researchers like John Bowlby and Mary Ainsworth have developed comprehensive models of attachment, highlighting how early relationships with caregivers influence adult romantic attachments.

Conclusion

The historical perspectives on the study of human attraction reveal a rich tapestry of evolving theories and insights. From ancient mythology and philosophy to modern interdisciplinary research, our understanding of attraction has grown more nuanced and sophisticated over the centuries. Each era has contributed unique perspectives, reflecting the changing social, cultural, and scientific contexts of the times.

As we continue to explore the complex interplay of biology, psychology, and sociology in attraction, we gain not only a deeper understanding of this fundamental human experience but also the tools to enrich our relationships and navigate the intricate dance of love with greater awareness and empathy. The journey of studying attraction is far from over, promising exciting discoveries and profound insights in the years to come.

CHAPTER 02

THE BIOLOGY OF ATTRACTION

Exploring the Role of Neurotransmitters: Dopamine, Serotonin, and Oxytocin

Attraction is not just an abstract emotional experience; it has a profound biological basis rooted in the brain's chemistry. Understanding the roles of neurotransmitters like dopamine, serotonin, and oxytocin provides critical insights into the mechanisms that drive romantic and sexual attraction.

Dopamine: The Pleasure and Reward Neurotransmitter

Dopamine is a key player in the brain's reward system, heavily involved in the feelings of pleasure and reinforcement. It plays a crucial role in the initial stages of attraction, often responsible for the euphoria and heightened energy we feel when we are infatuated with someone.

The Dopamine Pathway:

The release of dopamine occurs in several areas of the brain, including the ventral tegmental area (VTA), the nucleus accumbens, and the prefrontal cortex. These areas are collectively known as the brain's reward pathway. When we experience something pleasurable, such as seeing someone we are attracted to, the brain releases dopamine, reinforcing the desire to seek out that experience again.

The Role in Romantic Attraction:

When two people are attracted to each other, the sight, sound, or even thought of the other person can trigger a surge of dopamine. This leads to the exhilarating feelings often associated with new love—intense happiness, increased energy, and a focus on the loved one. Studies using functional magnetic resonance imaging (fMRI) have shown that when people look at pictures of their romantic partners, there is significant activation in the brain's dopamine-rich areas.

Dopamine and Risk-Taking:

Dopamine is also linked to risk-taking behaviors. In the context of attraction, this can manifest as taking bold steps to attract a potential mate or engaging in activities that might seem out of character. This is part of the brain's way of pushing us toward actions that could lead to romantic or sexual success.

Serotonin: The Mood Stabilizer

While dopamine ramps up our energy and focus during attraction, serotonin helps to balance our moods and regulate our emotional responses. However, during the early stages of intense romantic attraction, serotonin levels can actually drop, which is thought to contribute to the obsessive thinking and behavior often seen in new lovers.

Serotonin's Role in Mood Regulation:

Serotonin is a neurotransmitter that significantly influences mood, emotion, and sleep. It is produced in the brain and the intestines and plays a crucial role in maintaining a sense of well-being and happiness. Low levels of serotonin are associated with mood disorders like depression and anxiety.

The Serotonin Dip in New Love:

Research has shown that people in the throes of early romantic attraction have lower levels of serotonin, similar to those observed in people with obsessive-compulsive disorder. This dip in serotonin can explain why new lovers often become preoccupied with their partners, constantly thinking about them and craving their presence. The lower serotonin levels heighten the sense of novelty and excitement but also contribute to the emotional rollercoaster that new love can bring.

Long-Term Relationships and Serotonin:

As relationships progress and stabilize, serotonin levels typically return to normal. This helps to shift the relationship from the intense, obsessive phase of early attraction to a more stable and enduring bond. Normalized serotonin levels support feelings of contentment and emotional stability, which are crucial for long-term relationship satisfaction.

Oxytocin: The Bonding Hormone

Oxytocin, often referred to as the "love hormone" or "cuddle hormone," plays a central role in forming and maintaining bonds between individuals. It is released in response to physical touch, such as hugging, kissing, and sexual activity, and it fosters feelings of closeness and attachment.

Oxytocin and Physical Intimacy:

Physical interactions like hugging, kissing, and sexual intercourse trigger the release of oxytocin from the pituitary gland. This hormone then acts on the brain to promote bonding and trust between individuals. For instance, higher levels of oxytocin have been linked to increased feelings of trust and emotional closeness in couples.

Maternal Bonding:

Oxytocin is well known for its role in childbirth and maternal behaviors. During labor, oxytocin levels spike, facilitating contractions and promoting bonding between mother and child. After birth, breastfeeding further stimulates oxytocin release, strengthening the mother-infant bond. This same bonding mechanism operates in romantic relationships, reinforcing the connection between partners.

Oxytocin and Long-Term Relationships:

In long-term relationships, oxytocin helps to maintain the bond between partners. Regular physical affection and sexual intimacy keep oxytocin levels elevated, supporting emotional connection and relationship satisfaction. Research has shown that couples with higher oxytocin levels tend to report greater relationship happiness and stability.

The Interplay of Dopamine, Serotonin, and Oxytocin

The interactions between dopamine, serotonin, and oxytocin create a complex neurochemical dance that drives human attraction and bonding. Each neurotransmitter plays a distinct yet interconnected role in the different stages of romantic relationships.

Initial Attraction:

In the early stages of attraction, dopamine takes center stage, creating feelings of pleasure and excitement. The drop in serotonin contributes to the obsessive focus on the new partner, while oxytocin begins to build the foundation for emotional bonding through physical touch.

Developing Relationship:

As the relationship develops, the intense dopamine-driven excitement may taper off, but serotonin levels stabilize, supporting a balanced mood. Oxytocin continues to strengthen the bond through ongoing physical and emotional intimacy.

Long-Term Bonding:

In long-term relationships, the steady presence of oxytocin fosters deep emotional connections and trust. Dopamine still plays a role, but in a more balanced way, contributing to ongoing pleasure and reinforcement of the relationship. Serotonin supports overall emotional well-being, helping to sustain a stable and satisfying partnership.

Conclusion

The biology of attraction is a testament to the intricate workings of the human brain. Neurotransmitters like dopamine, serotonin, and oxytocin orchestrate the complex processes that drive romantic and sexual attraction, each contributing uniquely to the experience. Understanding these biochemical foundations not only enriches our knowledge of human behavior but also offers valuable insights into fostering healthy and fulfilling relationships.

As we continue to explore the depths of our neurobiology, we uncover more about the fundamental nature of love and attraction. This knowledge empowers us to navigate our relationships with greater awareness, compassion, and intentionality, ultimately enhancing the human experience of love and connection.

THE BIOLOGY OF ATTRACTION

How Hormones Such as Testosterone and Estrogen Influence Attraction

Hormones play a critical role in the complex interplay of factors that drive human attraction. Among the most influential hormones are testosterone and estrogen, which are fundamental to the development and regulation of sexual attraction and behavior. These hormones not only shape physical and behavioral characteristics but also significantly impact how individuals perceive and respond to potential mates.

Testosterone: The Hormone of Desire

Testosterone, often dubbed the "male hormone," is produced primarily in the testes in men and in smaller amounts in the ovaries in women. Despite its reputation as a male hormone, testosterone plays a crucial role in both genders, influencing libido, energy levels, and assertive behaviors.

Testosterone and Male Attraction:

In men, testosterone levels are linked to the intensity of sexual desire and attraction. Higher testosterone levels often correlate with an increased libido and a greater likelihood of pursuing potential mates. This hormone drives behaviors that enhance mating success, such as competitiveness, dominance, and risk-taking. Men with higher testosterone levels may exhibit more pronounced secondary sexual characteristics, like increased muscle mass and facial hair, which can make them more attractive to potential partners.

Testosterone and Female Attraction:

Although women have lower levels of testosterone compared to men, this hormone still plays a significant role in female sexual attraction and behavior. Testosterone influences women's sexual desire and can affect their receptiveness to potential mates. Research suggests that women with higher testosterone levels may experience stronger sexual desire and may be more assertive in seeking romantic relationships. Additionally, fluctuations in testosterone levels during the menstrual cycle can impact women's attraction to certain traits in men, such as facial symmetry and physical strength.

Testosterone's Role in Partner Selection:

Testosterone also affects how individuals select their partners. Men with higher testosterone levels may prioritize physical attractiveness and youth in their mates, traits that are often associated with fertility. In contrast, women may find men with higher testosterone levels more attractive during certain phases of their menstrual cycle, particularly when they are ovulating and their reproductive potential is at its peak.

Estrogen: The Hormone of Femininity and Attraction

Estrogen, often considered the "female hormone," is primarily produced in the ovaries in women and in smaller amounts in the testes in men. Estrogen is essential for the development of female secondary sexual characteristics and plays a significant role in regulating the menstrual cycle and reproductive system.

Estrogen and Female Attraction:

In women, estrogen levels influence a range of behaviors and traits related to attraction. Higher estrogen levels are associated with increased fertility, which can make women more attractive to potential mates. Estrogen contributes to the development of physical features often deemed attractive, such as a youthful appearance, clear skin, and a lower waist-to-hip ratio. During the ovulatory phase of the menstrual cycle, when estrogen levels peak, women may experience heightened sexual desire and increased attraction to potential partners.

Estrogen and Male Attraction:

Men are subconsciously attuned to cues of high estrogen levels in women, as these signals indicate fertility and reproductive potential. Studies have shown that men find women with higher estrogen levels more attractive, particularly during their ovulatory phase. These cues can include changes in a woman's scent, voice, and even behavior, which can subtly signal her increased fertility to potential mates.

Estrogen's Role in Partner Selection:

Estrogen influences women's preferences for certain traits in men, such as social status, resources, and emotional stability. These preferences can vary throughout the menstrual cycle, with women showing a stronger preference for masculine features and behaviors during ovulation. This cyclical variation in attraction highlights the dynamic interplay between hormonal levels and mate selection.

The Synergy of Testosterone and Estrogen

The interplay between testosterone and estrogen is not only crucial within individuals but also affects the dynamics of attraction between partners. The balance and interaction of these hormones shape how men and women perceive each other and how they behave in romantic and sexual contexts.

Mutual Attraction:

The mutual influence of testosterone and estrogen can enhance the overall attraction between partners. For instance, high testosterone levels in men may lead to behaviors that signal confidence and dominance, which can be attractive to women, especially when their estrogen levels are high. Similarly, the physical and behavioral cues associated with high estrogen levels in women can make them more appealing to men, whose testosterone-driven attraction to these cues enhances mutual desire.

Hormonal Synchrony:

Hormonal synchrony, where partners' hormone levels influence each other, can also play a role in attraction and relationship satisfaction. Studies have shown that couples in close, intimate relationships can experience synchronized hormonal changes, which can enhance emotional bonding and sexual attraction. This hormonal interplay reinforces the connection between partners, contributing to a stable and satisfying relationship.

The Evolutionary Perspective

From an evolutionary standpoint, the roles of testosterone and estrogen in attraction make sense as mechanisms that enhance reproductive success. Traits and behaviors influenced by these hormones often signal genetic fitness and reproductive potential, making individuals more attractive to potential mates.

Sexual Selection:

Sexual selection, a form of natural selection, explains how certain traits become more prevalent in a population because they are deemed attractive by the opposite sex. Testosterone-driven traits in men, such as physical strength and assertiveness, can signal genetic fitness and the ability to provide and protect. Estrogen-driven traits in women, such as fertility indicators and nurturing behaviors, signal reproductive potential and the ability to care for offspring.

Mate Preferences:

The hormonal basis of attraction also helps explain why certain traits are universally attractive across cultures. For example, the preference for youthful appearance and clear skin in women and the preference for physical strength and social status in men are rooted in the reproductive advantages these traits confer.

Conclusion

Hormones like testosterone and estrogen are powerful drivers of human attraction, influencing not only our physical traits but also our behaviors and preferences. Understanding the roles of these hormones provides valuable insights into the biological foundations of attraction and the evolutionary forces that shape our romantic and sexual lives.

As we delve deeper into the science of attraction, we gain a greater appreciation for the intricate mechanisms that underlie this fundamental aspect of human experience. This knowledge can enrich our understanding of relationships, helping us navigate the complexities of love and desire with greater awareness and empathy. The biological perspective on attraction is just one piece of the puzzle, but it offers a crucial lens through which we can better understand the profound connections that bind us together.

GENETIC FACTORS AND THEIR IMPACT ON MATE SELECTION

Genetic factors play a crucial role in shaping human attraction and mate selection. Our genetic makeup influences not only our physical appearance and health but also our preferences and behaviors when it comes to choosing a partner. This chapter explores the various ways in which genetics impact mate selection, shedding light on the complex interplay between our biological inheritance and our romantic choices.

The Role of Genetic Compatibility

One of the most significant aspects of genetic influence on mate selection is the concept of genetic compatibility. Humans have evolved mechanisms to select mates whose genetic makeup complements their own, enhancing the chances of producing healthy offspring.

Major Histocompatibility Complex (MHC):

The Major Histocompatibility Complex (MHC) is a set of genes crucial for immune system function. Research has shown that individuals are often attracted to mates with different MHC genes than their own. This preference is thought to increase the genetic diversity of offspring, enhancing their immune system's ability to combat a wider range of pathogens. Studies involving body odor and sweat samples have demonstrated that people tend to find the scent of those with dissimilar MHC genes more attractive, indicating a subconscious mechanism for detecting genetic compatibility.

Inbreeding Avoidance:

Genetic factors also play a role in avoiding inbreeding, which can lead to the expression of harmful recessive genes. Humans, like many other animals, have evolved to recognize and avoid mating with close relatives. This avoidance is thought to be partly mediated by genetic cues, such as scent and facial features, which signal relatedness.

Physical Traits and Genetic Signals

Our genes significantly influence our physical appearance, and these traits can serve as signals of genetic fitness to potential mates. Certain physical characteristics are universally perceived as attractive because they indicate good health and reproductive potential.

Facial Symmetry:

Facial symmetry is often associated with genetic health and developmental stability. Symmetrical faces are perceived as more attractive across different cultures, likely because they signal an individual's ability to withstand environmental stresses during development. Studies have shown that people with symmetrical faces are often rated as more attractive and are more likely to be chosen as mates.

Sexual Dimorphism:

Sexual dimorphism refers to the differences in appearance between males and females of a species. In humans, features such as a strong jawline and broad shoulders in men, and a low waist-to-hip ratio and fuller lips in women, are often seen as attractive. These traits are influenced by sex hormones like testosterone and estrogen, which in turn are regulated by our genes. Sexual dimorphism signals fertility and reproductive health, making these traits desirable in potential mates.

Skin Quality:

Skin quality is another physical trait influenced by genetics that impacts mate selection. Clear, smooth skin is often perceived as a sign of health and youthfulness, both of which are desirable traits in a mate. Genetic factors contribute to skin quality by regulating processes such as collagen production and skin repair mechanisms.

Genetic Influence on Behavior and Preferences

Beyond physical traits, genetics also influence behaviors and preferences related to mate selection. These behavioral traits can impact how we choose partners and how we behave within relationships.

Mate Preferences:

Genetic factors can shape our preferences for certain traits in potential mates. For example, some studies suggest that individuals may have a genetic predisposition to prefer mates with specific personality traits, such as extraversion or agreeableness. These preferences can enhance compatibility and relationship satisfaction.

Risk-Taking and Sensation-Seeking:

Genes also influence personality traits such as risk-taking and sensation-seeking, which can affect mate selection. Individuals with higher levels of these traits may be more likely to pursue multiple partners or seek out novel experiences, impacting their romantic choices. These behaviors are thought to be influenced by genetic variations in neurotransmitter systems, such as the dopamine system.

Attachment Styles:

Attachment styles, which describe how individuals form and maintain relationships, are also influenced by genetics. Research has shown that genetic factors contribute to individual differences in attachment styles, such as secure, anxious, or avoidant attachment. These styles can affect mate selection by influencing how individuals perceive and respond to potential partners.

Evolutionary Perspectives on Genetic Factors in Mate Selection

From an evolutionary perspective, the influence of genetic factors on mate selection makes sense as a strategy to enhance reproductive success. By choosing mates with complementary or advantageous genetic traits, individuals increase the likelihood of producing healthy, viable offspring.

Parental Investment Theory:

Parental investment theory posits that the sex that invests more in offspring (typically females) will be more selective in mate choice, while the sex that invests less (typically males) will compete for access to the more selective sex. This theory explains many observed patterns of mate selection and attraction, including the importance of genetic traits that signal health and reproductive potential.

Mate Competition:

Mate competition drives the evolution of traits that enhance an individual's attractiveness and competitiveness. For example, men may evolve traits like physical strength and social dominance to outcompete rivals, while women may evolve traits like youthfulness and beauty to attract high-quality mates. These traits are influenced by genetic factors and are subject to sexual selection pressures.

Genetic Research and Modern Implications

Advances in genetic research have provided new insights into the role of genetics in mate selection. Techniques such as genome-wide association studies (GWAS) and twin studies have helped identify specific genes and genetic variants associated with traits related to attraction and mate choice.

Genome-Wide Association Studies:

GWAS involve scanning the genomes of large populations to identify genetic variations associated with specific traits. These studies have identified genetic variants linked to physical traits like height and facial structure, as well as behavioral traits like personality and risk-taking.

Twin Studies:

Twin studies, which compare the similarities between identical and fraternal twins, have been instrumental in estimating the heritability of traits related to attraction. These studies have shown that many traits influencing mate selection, such as physical attractiveness and personality, have a significant genetic component.

Implications for Modern Society:

Understanding the genetic basis of mate selection has implications for modern society, including the fields of psychology, medicine, and relationship counseling. This knowledge can help individuals make informed decisions about their romantic relationships and address issues related to compatibility and reproductive health.

Conclusion

Genetic factors play a pivotal role in shaping human attraction and mate selection. From physical traits and genetic compatibility to behaviors and preferences, our genes influence how we perceive and choose potential mates. These genetic influences are rooted in evolutionary strategies designed to enhance reproductive success and ensure the survival of our species.

As we continue to explore the genetic basis of attraction, we gain valuable insights into the biological foundations of human relationships. This knowledge not only enriches our understanding of attraction but also empowers us to navigate the complexities of love and mate selection with greater awareness and intentionality. The interplay between genetics and attraction is a testament to the intricate and multifaceted nature of human love, offering a fascinating glimpse into the forces that drive our deepest connections.

CHAPTER 03

THE PSYCHOLOGY OF ATTRACTION

Freudian and Jungian Perspectives on Attraction

The psychological aspects of attraction are complex and multifaceted, encompassing a wide range of theories and perspectives. Among the most influential are the psychoanalytic theories developed by Sigmund Freud and Carl Jung. These perspectives provide deep insights into the unconscious factors and archetypal patterns that shape human attraction.

Freudian Perspective on Attraction

Sigmund Freud, the founder of psychoanalysis, introduced groundbreaking ideas about the unconscious mind and its influence on human behavior, including attraction. Freud's theories emphasize the role of unconscious desires, childhood experiences, and psychosexual development in shaping our romantic and sexual preferences.

The Unconscious Mind:

Freud believed that much of human behavior is driven by unconscious desires and motivations. He proposed that the mind is divided into three parts: the id, the ego, and the superego. The id represents our primal, instinctual drives, including sexual and aggressive urges. The ego mediates between the desires of the id and the constraints of reality, while the superego represents internalized societal norms and morals.

In the context of attraction, Freud argued that unconscious desires originating from the id play a significant role. These desires are often influenced by repressed childhood experiences and unresolved conflicts.

Psychosexual Development:

Freud's theory of psychosexual development posits that individuals pass through a series of stages during childhood, each characterized by the focus of libido (sexual energy) on different erogenous zones. These stages are the oral, anal, phallic, latent, and genital stages.

- Oral Stage: In the first year of life, the mouth is the primary source of pleasure. Fixations at this stage can lead to traits such as dependency or aggression.

- Anal Stage: During the second and third years, pleasure centers on bowel and bladder control. Fixations here can result in obsessiveness or messiness.

- Phallic Stage: From ages three to six, the focus shifts to the genitals. This stage is crucial for the development of sexual identity and attraction. Freud introduced the concepts of the Oedipus complex (in boys) and the Electra complex (in girls), where children experience unconscious sexual desires for the opposite-sex parent and rivalry with the same-sex parent.

- Latency Stage: From age six to puberty, sexual impulses are repressed, allowing for the development of social and intellectual skills.

- Genital Stage: Beginning at puberty, sexual impulses reawaken, and individuals seek to form mature sexual relationships.

Freud believed that fixations or unresolved conflicts at any of these stages could influence adult romantic preferences and behaviors. For example, unresolved Oedipal or Electra complexes could lead to individuals seeking partners who resemble their opposite-sex parent.

Defense Mechanisms:

Freud also identified defense mechanisms as unconscious strategies used by the ego to manage anxiety and internal conflict. In the context of attraction, defense mechanisms such as projection, displacement, and sublimation can play a role. For instance, individuals might project their own unacceptable desires onto others or displace their romantic feelings onto more socially acceptable targets.

Jungian Perspective on Attraction

Carl Jung, a former disciple of Freud who later developed his own school of thought, introduced several key concepts that have profoundly influenced our understanding of attraction. Jung's theories focus on the collective unconscious, archetypes, and the process of individuation.

The Collective Unconscious:

Jung proposed the existence of a collective unconscious, a deeper layer of the unconscious mind shared by all humans. This collective unconscious contains universal archetypes, which are innate, symbolic representations that influence our behaviors and experiences.

In terms of attraction, the collective unconscious and its archetypes shape our perceptions and preferences. Archetypes such as the Anima and Animus, the Shadow, and the Self play crucial roles in romantic attraction.

Anima and Animus:

The Anima and Animus are key Jungian concepts related to attraction. The Anima represents the feminine aspect within the male psyche, while the Animus represents the masculine aspect within the female psyche. Jung believed that these archetypes influence how individuals perceive and interact with the opposite sex.

- Anima: In men, the Anima is often projected onto women, shaping their romantic ideals and preferences. A man's Anima might lead him to seek partners who embody his inner feminine qualities, such as sensitivity, intuition, and nurturing.

- Animus: In women, the Animus is projected onto men, influencing their romantic choices. A woman's Animus might draw her to partners who exhibit her inner masculine traits, such as assertiveness, intellect, and strength.

Jung suggested that healthy relationships involve recognizing and integrating these projections, leading to a more balanced and authentic connection with the partner.

The Shadow:

The Shadow represents the parts of the self that are repressed or denied. It contains both negative and positive traits that the individual has not integrated into their conscious personality. In the context of attraction, the Shadow can influence romantic preferences by drawing individuals to partners who embody their repressed qualities.

For example, someone who represses their assertiveness might be attracted to a partner who is highly assertive. This attraction can be a way for the individual to confront and integrate their Shadow traits. However, it can also lead to conflicts if the repressed qualities are projected onto the partner in a negative way.

Individuation and Attraction:

Individuation is the process of integrating various aspects of the self to achieve psychological wholeness. Jung believed that romantic relationships could facilitate individuation by providing opportunities to confront and integrate unconscious aspects of the self.

Attraction to a partner often involves encountering parts of the self that are unfamiliar or repressed. Through the relationship, individuals can achieve greater self-awareness and personal growth. The challenges and conflicts that arise in relationships can be seen as opportunities for individuation, leading to a more complete and balanced self.

Comparing Freudian and Jungian Perspectives

While both Freud and Jung emphasize the influence of the unconscious mind on attraction, their approaches differ in several key ways:

Focus on Childhood vs. Collective Unconscious:

Freud's theories focus heavily on the impact of early childhood experiences and psychosexual development on adult attraction. He believed that unresolved conflicts from these stages shape our romantic preferences and behaviors. In contrast, Jung's theories emphasize the collective unconscious and archetypes, suggesting that universal symbols and patterns influence attraction.

Defense Mechanisms vs. Archetypes:

Freud's concept of defense mechanisms highlights the ways in which the ego manages unconscious desires and conflicts. These mechanisms can influence how individuals experience and express attraction. Jung, on the other hand, focuses on archetypes like the Anima, Animus, and Shadow, which shape our perceptions and interactions with potential partners.

Individuation:

Jung's concept of individuation adds a unique dimension to the understanding of attraction. He sees romantic relationships as opportunities for personal growth and self-integration. Freud's theories, while acknowledging the influence of unconscious desires, do not emphasize this process of achieving psychological wholeness through relationships.

Conclusion

Freudian and Jungian perspectives on attraction offer valuable insights into the deep, unconscious factors that shape our romantic and sexual preferences. Freud's emphasis on early childhood experiences and psychosexual development highlights the lasting impact of formative years on adult attraction. Jung's focus on the collective unconscious and archetypal patterns provides a broader, more universal framework for understanding the dynamics of attraction.

Together, these perspectives enrich our understanding of the psychological underpinnings of attraction, revealing the intricate interplay between our unconscious mind, personal history, and universal human experiences. By exploring these theories, we gain a deeper appreciation for the complexities of human attraction and the profound forces that draw us toward one another.

ATTACHMENT THEORY AND ITS RELEVANCE TO ROMANTIC RELATIONSHIPS

Attachment theory, developed by John Bowlby and later expanded by Mary Ainsworth, is one of the most influential frameworks in understanding human relationships. It provides a comprehensive explanation of how early interactions with primary caregivers shape our patterns of attachment and influence our behavior in romantic relationships. This chapter explores the key concepts of attachment theory and their relevance to romantic attraction and relationships.

Origins of Attachment Theory

John Bowlby, a British psychologist, was the first to propose attachment theory in the mid-20th century. His work was grounded in the idea that children are biologically predisposed to form attachments with their caregivers as a means of survival. Bowlby argued that the quality of these early attachments significantly influences a person's emotional and social development.

Mary Ainsworth, an American-Canadian developmental psychologist, further developed Bowlby's ideas through her famous "Strange Situation" experiments. These experiments observed how infants reacted to separation and reunion with their caregivers, leading to the identification of different attachment styles.

Key Concepts of Attachment Theory

Attachment Styles:

Ainsworth's research identified three primary attachment styles in infants: secure, anxious-ambivalent, and avoidant. Later research added a fourth style: disorganized. These attachment styles are thought to persist into adulthood, influencing romantic relationships.

1. Secure Attachment:

- Characteristics: Individuals with a secure attachment style generally feel comfortable with intimacy and independence. They tend to have positive views of themselves and others, are able to form healthy, trusting relationships, and are comfortable relying on others and being relied upon.

- Influence on Relationships: Securely attached individuals are likely to have healthier and more satisfying romantic relationships. They can communicate effectively, manage conflicts constructively, and provide emotional support to their partners.

2. Anxious-Ambivalent Attachment:

- Characteristics: Individuals with an anxious-ambivalent attachment style often crave closeness and approval but are worried about their partner's availability and commitment. They may be overly dependent on their partners and experience intense fear of abandonment.

- Influence on Relationships: Anxiously attached individuals may struggle with insecurity and jealousy in relationships. They might demand constant reassurance and display clingy or needy behaviors, which can strain the relationship.

3. Avoidant Attachment:

- Characteristics: Individuals with an avoidant attachment style tend to distance themselves from others to avoid dependency and intimacy. They often value independence and self-sufficiency, sometimes at the expense of close relationships.

- Influence on Relationships: Avoidantly attached individuals may have difficulty forming deep connections and can appear emotionally distant. They may avoid vulnerability and struggle with expressing their feelings, leading to challenges in maintaining intimate relationships.

4. Disorganized Attachment:

- Characteristics: Individuals with a disorganized attachment style display a mix of anxious and avoidant behaviors. This style often arises from inconsistent or traumatic caregiving experiences.

- Influence on Relationships: Disorganized attachment can lead to erratic and unpredictable behavior in relationships. These individuals may have difficulty trusting others and regulating their emotions, which can result in turbulent and unstable relationships.

Attachment Theory in Adult Romantic Relationships

The principles of attachment theory extend beyond childhood, influencing adult romantic relationships in several ways. Understanding one's attachment style can provide valuable insights into relationship dynamics and help individuals develop healthier patterns of interaction.

Formation of Romantic Relationships:

Attachment styles influence how individuals approach and form romantic relationships. Securely attached individuals are more likely to seek out and establish stable, fulfilling partnerships. Anxiously attached individuals may rush into relationships seeking reassurance, while avoidantly attached individuals might delay or avoid commitment altogether.

Behavior in Relationships:

Attachment styles shape behavior within romantic relationships, affecting communication, conflict resolution, and emotional intimacy. Secure individuals typically communicate openly and effectively, while anxious individuals may display heightened sensitivity to perceived threats to the relationship. Avoidant individuals might withdraw during conflicts, preferring to handle issues independently rather than collaboratively.

Response to Relationship Stress:

Attachment styles also influence how individuals respond to stress and challenges in relationships. Securely attached individuals are more likely to seek and offer support during difficult times, enhancing relationship resilience.

Anxiously attached individuals might react with heightened anxiety and demand reassurance, whereas avoidantly attached individuals may detach emotionally to cope with stress.

Impact on Relationship Satisfaction:

Research consistently shows that secure attachment is associated with higher relationship satisfaction and stability. Secure individuals report greater emotional closeness, trust, and mutual support in their relationships. In contrast, anxious and avoidant attachment styles are linked to lower relationship satisfaction, higher conflict levels, and increased risk of relationship dissolution.

The Role of Attachment in Partner Selection

Attachment theory provides a framework for understanding how individuals select their partners based on their attachment styles. People tend to be drawn to partners who complement their attachment needs, although this can sometimes lead to maladaptive patterns.

Attachment Matching:

Securely attached individuals often seek and attract partners who are also secure, leading to balanced and healthy relationships. However, individuals with insecure attachment styles (anxious or avoidant) may unconsciously seek partners who reinforce their existing attachment patterns. For example, an anxiously attached person might be drawn to an avoidantly attached partner, creating a cycle of pursuit and withdrawal that perpetuates their insecurities.

Attachment and Relationship Dynamics:

Understanding attachment styles can help individuals recognize and address unhealthy relationship dynamics. For example, an anxiously attached person can work on developing self-reliance and reducing their need for constant reassurance, while an avoidantly attached person can practice emotional openness and vulnerability.

Attachment and Therapy:

Attachment theory has significant implications for relationship therapy and counseling. Therapists can help individuals and couples understand their attachment styles and develop strategies to improve their relationship dynamics. Interventions may include building emotional awareness, enhancing communication skills, and fostering secure attachment behaviors.

Changing Attachment Patterns

While attachment styles are relatively stable, they are not immutable. Individuals can develop more secure attachment patterns through self-awareness, personal growth, and therapeutic interventions.

Self-Reflection and Awareness:

Understanding one's attachment style is the first step toward change. Self-reflection and awareness can help individuals recognize how their attachment patterns influence their behavior and relationships. Journaling, introspection, and discussing attachment experiences with trusted friends or therapists can facilitate this process.

Building Secure Attachment:

Individuals can work on building secure attachment behaviors by developing trust, improving communication skills, and practicing emotional regulation. Building secure attachment often involves addressing past traumas, resolving unresolved conflicts, and fostering positive relationship experiences.

Therapeutic Interventions:

Therapy can be a powerful tool for changing attachment patterns. Therapists can help individuals explore their attachment histories, understand their current relationship dynamics, and develop healthier ways of relating to others. Approaches such as Emotionally Focused Therapy (EFT) and Attachment-Based Therapy can be particularly effective in addressing attachment issues.

Conclusion

Attachment theory offers a profound understanding of how early experiences with caregivers shape our patterns of attachment and influence our romantic relationships. By identifying and addressing attachment styles, individuals can gain insights into their relationship behaviors and work toward developing healthier, more secure attachments.

The relevance of attachment theory to romantic relationships underscores the importance of emotional bonds and the lasting impact of early experiences. As we navigate the complexities of love and connection, understanding attachment theory can empower us to build more fulfilling and resilient relationships, enhancing our overall well-being and happiness.

COGNITIVE BIASES AND THEIR INFLUENCE ON ATTRACTION

Human attraction is not solely driven by rational decisions and conscious choices; it is significantly influenced by cognitive biases. These biases are systematic patterns of deviation from rationality in judgment, leading us to make decisions and form perceptions in ways that are often irrational but predictable. Understanding these cognitive biases can provide valuable insights into why we are attracted to certain individuals and how these biases shape our romantic relationships.

The Halo Effect

One of the most well-documented cognitive biases influencing attraction is the halo effect. This bias occurs when our overall impression of a person influences how we perceive their specific traits. For example, if we find someone physically attractive, we are more likely to assume they possess other positive qualities, such as kindness, intelligence, and competence.

Impact on Attraction:

The halo effect can lead us to overestimate the positive attributes of someone we find attractive. This can result in an idealized view of the person, making us more likely to pursue a relationship with them based on these inflated perceptions. While the halo effect can enhance initial attraction, it can also lead to disappointment if the person does not meet our elevated expectations over time.

Confirmation Bias

Confirmation bias is the tendency to seek out, interpret, and remember information that confirms our preexisting beliefs and attitudes while ignoring or discounting information that contradicts them. In the context of attraction, confirmation bias can influence how we perceive and interact with potential partners.

Impact on Attraction:

When we are attracted to someone, we are more likely to notice and remember their positive traits and behaviors, reinforcing our initial attraction. Conversely, we might overlook or rationalize their negative traits and behaviors. This bias can make us more confident in our choice of partner, but it can also blind us to potential red flags in the relationship.

Similarity Bias

The similarity bias is the tendency to be attracted to people who are similar to us in terms of interests, values, beliefs, and background. This bias is rooted in the comfort and validation that comes from being with someone who shares our worldview and experiences.

Impact on Attraction:

Similarity bias can lead to stronger initial attraction and bonding, as shared interests and values provide common ground for connection. Relationships formed on the basis of similarity often experience higher levels of satisfaction and stability. However, this bias can also limit our exposure to diverse perspectives and experiences, potentially leading to a more homogenous social and romantic life.

Mere Exposure Effect

The mere exposure effect, also known as the familiarity principle, is the tendency to develop a preference for things or people we are exposed to frequently. This bias suggests that repeated exposure to a person increases our likelihood of being attracted to them.

Impact on Attraction:

The mere exposure effect can influence attraction by making us more comfortable and familiar with someone, which can enhance feelings of affection and attachment. This is why proximity and frequent interactions, such as those with coworkers or classmates, often lead to romantic relationships. However, overexposure without positive interactions can lead to boredom or irritation, highlighting the need for a balance between familiarity and novelty.

Reciprocity of Liking

The reciprocity of liking is the tendency to be attracted to people who express liking for us. This bias is based on the positive reinforcement we receive when someone shows interest in us, boosting our self-esteem and encouraging mutual attraction.

Impact on Attraction:

Knowing that someone is attracted to us can increase our attraction to them, creating a positive feedback loop that fosters mutual interest. This bias can help initiate and sustain romantic relationships, as mutual liking is a strong foundation for connection. However, it can also lead to attraction based on the need for validation rather than genuine compatibility.

The Sunk Cost Fallacy

The sunk cost fallacy is the tendency to continue investing in a relationship based on the time, effort, and resources already invested, rather than evaluating the current and future benefits of the relationship. This bias can lead to staying in unfulfilling or unhealthy relationships due to the reluctance to "waste" past investments.

Impact on Attraction:

The sunk cost fallacy can make us more committed to a relationship even when it no longer serves our best interests. This bias can result in staying with a partner out of a sense of obligation or fear of losing what we have invested, rather than genuine attraction or compatibility. Recognizing this bias can help individuals make more rational decisions about their relationships.

The Pygmalion Effect

The Pygmalion effect, also known as the self-fulfilling prophecy, is the phenomenon where our expectations about someone can influence their behavior to align with those expectations. In romantic relationships, this bias can shape how partners perceive and respond to each other.

Impact on Attraction:

Positive expectations about a partner can enhance their self-esteem and encourage behaviors that fulfill those expectations, strengthening the relationship. Conversely, negative expectations can lead to behaviors that undermine the relationship. Being aware of the Pygmalion effect can help individuals foster positive dynamics in their relationships by maintaining supportive and encouraging expectations.

Loss Aversion

Loss aversion is the tendency to prefer avoiding losses over acquiring equivalent gains. In the context of attraction, this bias can influence how we perceive and respond to potential threats to a relationship.

Impact on Attraction:

Loss aversion can make individuals more sensitive to signs of potential relationship breakdown and more motivated to avoid or mitigate those threats. This bias can enhance commitment and efforts to maintain the relationship. However, it can also lead to excessive fear of loss and unhealthy attachment behaviors, such as jealousy and possessiveness.

The Anchoring Effect

The anchoring effect is the cognitive bias where an initial piece of information (the "anchor") influences subsequent judgments and decisions. In romantic relationships, the first impressions and early experiences can serve as anchors that shape our perception of a partner.

Impact on Attraction:

First impressions and initial encounters can heavily influence our overall perception of a partner, affecting how we interpret their later behaviors and traits. Positive early experiences can create a favorable anchor, making us more forgiving of later imperfections. Conversely, negative anchors can bias us against fully appreciating a partner's positive qualities. Being aware of the anchoring effect can help individuals reassess their perceptions and avoid undue influence from initial biases.

Conclusion

Cognitive biases play a significant role in shaping human attraction and romantic relationships. By understanding these biases, individuals can gain insights into their own behaviors and perceptions, leading to more mindful and informed decisions in their romantic lives.

Recognizing the influence of cognitive biases can help individuals navigate the complexities of attraction with greater awareness and intentionality. By addressing these biases, we can foster healthier, more authentic relationships, grounded in genuine connection rather than distorted perceptions. The interplay between cognitive biases and attraction underscores the intricate nature of human relationships, highlighting the importance of both psychological awareness and emotional intelligence in the pursuit of lasting love and fulfillment.

54

CHAPTER 04

LOVE AND THE BRAIN

Neurological Processes Involved in Falling in Love

Love is often described as a profound emotional experience, but at its core, it is also a complex neurological process. When we fall in love, a cascade of brain activity and chemical reactions orchestrates the feelings of euphoria, attachment, and bonding that characterize romantic relationships. This chapter delves into the neurological processes involved in falling in love, exploring how different parts of the brain and various neurotransmitters work together to create the sensation of love.

The Brain's Reward System

Falling in love activates the brain's reward system, a network of structures involved in processing pleasure, motivation, and reinforcement. The primary components of this system include the ventral tegmental area (VTA), the nucleus accumbens, and the prefrontal cortex.

Ventral Tegmental Area (VTA):

The VTA is one of the first areas to become active when we fall in love. It produces dopamine, a neurotransmitter associated with pleasure and reward. When we see or think about our romantic partner, the VTA releases dopamine, creating feelings of excitement and happiness. This dopamine surge reinforces our desire to be close to our partner, motivating us to seek out and maintain the relationship.

Nucleus Accumbens:

The nucleus accumbens, part of the brain's reward circuitry, is heavily involved in the feelings of pleasure and reinforcement associated with romantic love. It receives dopamine signals from the VTA, amplifying the pleasurable sensations and reinforcing the behavior that triggered the dopamine release. This process makes us feel good when we are with our partner and encourages us to continue seeking their company.

Prefrontal Cortex:

The prefrontal cortex, responsible for higher-order cognitive functions such as decision-making and impulse control, also plays a role in romantic love. During the early stages of love, activity in the prefrontal cortex can decrease, leading to reduced critical thinking and increased impulsivity. This can explain why people often make bold or seemingly irrational decisions when they are in love.

The Role of Neurotransmitters

Several neurotransmitters are crucial in the neurological processes involved in falling in love. These chemical messengers facilitate communication between neurons, influencing our emotions, behaviors, and experiences of love.

Dopamine:

Dopamine is the primary neurotransmitter associated with the pleasure and reward aspects of love. Its release in response to romantic stimuli creates feelings of euphoria, excitement, and energy. High levels of dopamine can make individuals feel infatuated and intensely focused on their partner, often leading to obsessive thoughts and behaviors.

Oxytocin:

Oxytocin, often referred to as the "love hormone" or "cuddle hormone," plays a vital role in bonding and attachment. It is released during physical touch, such as hugging, kissing, and sexual activity, promoting feelings of closeness and trust. Oxytocin strengthens the emotional bond between partners, enhancing relationship stability and satisfaction.

Serotonin:

Serotonin is involved in mood regulation and emotional stability. During the early stages of romantic love, serotonin levels can decrease, contributing to the obsessive thinking and heightened anxiety often experienced by new lovers. Over time, as the relationship stabilizes, serotonin levels typically normalize, supporting a more balanced and enduring emotional connection.

Vasopressin:

Vasopressin, another hormone associated with social bonding, complements the effects of oxytocin. It plays a role in long-term commitment and monogamous behaviors. Studies on animals, such as prairie voles, have shown that vasopressin is critical for pair-bonding and partner preference, suggesting a similar function in humans.

Endorphins:

Endorphins, the body's natural painkillers, also contribute to the feelings of comfort and security in romantic relationships. They are released during physical affection and shared positive experiences, creating a sense of well-being and emotional stability.

Brain Regions Involved in Romantic Love

Various brain regions work together to create the experience of romantic love, each contributing unique functions and processes.

Amygdala:

The amygdala, involved in processing emotions and fear, shows decreased activity during romantic love. This reduction in activity may help explain why people in love often feel less fearful and more willing to take risks for their partner. The dampening of the amygdala's response can also lead to a greater sense of security and trust in the relationship.

Hippocampus:

The hippocampus, critical for memory formation, plays a role in storing and recalling emotional experiences with a romantic partner. Positive memories of time spent together can strengthen the emotional bond and reinforce feelings of love and attachment.

Anterior Cingulate Cortex:

The anterior cingulate cortex (ACC) is involved in emotional regulation and empathy. During romantic love, the ACC becomes more active, enhancing our ability to understand and share our partner's emotions. This increased empathy fosters deeper emotional connections and helps maintain relationship harmony.

Insula:

The insula, responsible for processing bodily sensations and emotional experiences, is also activated during romantic love. It integrates physical and emotional information, contributing to the intense feelings of connection and physical arousal experienced in love.

The Phases of Romantic Love

Romantic love can be divided into different phases, each characterized by distinct neurological processes and hormonal changes.

Lust:

The initial phase of romantic attraction is driven by sexual desire and the release of sex hormones, such as testosterone and estrogen. These hormones increase libido and motivate individuals to seek out potential mates. Lust is characterized by a strong physical attraction and the desire for sexual intimacy.

Attraction:

The attraction phase involves the intense infatuation and passion often experienced at the beginning of a romantic relationship. During this phase, dopamine, norepinephrine, and serotonin levels fluctuate, creating feelings of euphoria, excitement, and obsessive thinking about the partner. This phase is marked by heightened energy, loss of appetite, and difficulty sleeping.

Attachment:

The attachment phase represents the deep emotional bond that develops over time between romantic partners. Oxytocin and vasopressin play crucial roles in this phase, promoting long-term commitment and emotional stability. Attachment is characterized by feelings of comfort, security, and mutual support.

Love and Long-Term Relationships

In long-term relationships, the initial intensity of romantic love often evolves into a more stable and enduring bond. While the passionate feelings of the attraction phase may wane, the attachment phase strengthens, supported by the continued release of oxytocin and vasopressin.

Maintaining the Bond:

Maintaining a strong emotional bond in long-term relationships involves nurturing the connection through regular physical affection, communication, and shared positive experiences. The ongoing release of oxytocin and endorphins during these activities reinforces the bond and promotes relationship satisfaction.

Neural Plasticity:

Neural plasticity, the brain's ability to adapt and change in response to experiences, plays a role in sustaining long-term love. Couples who engage in novel and stimulating activities together can enhance neural plasticity, keeping the relationship dynamic and exciting.

Challenges in Long-Term Love:

Despite the strong bond formed during the attachment phase, long-term relationships can face challenges, such as stress, conflicts, and external pressures. Addressing these challenges requires effective communication, empathy, and mutual support. The brain's ability to adapt and the continued release of bonding hormones can help couples navigate these difficulties and maintain a healthy relationship.

Conclusion

Falling in love is a complex neurological process involving various brain regions and neurotransmitters. The brain's reward system, along with hormones such as dopamine, oxytocin, serotonin, and vasopressin, orchestrates the feelings of euphoria, attachment, and bonding that characterize romantic relationships.

Understanding the neurological processes involved in love provides valuable insights into the nature of human attraction and attachment. It highlights the profound impact of brain chemistry on our emotions and behaviors, offering a deeper appreciation for the intricacies of romantic relationships.

As we continue to explore the science of love, we gain a greater understanding of how to nurture and sustain healthy, fulfilling relationships. By recognizing the neurological underpinnings of love, we can navigate the complexities of romance with greater awareness and intentionality, enhancing our overall well-being and happiness.

THE SCIENCE BEHIND INFATUATION AND LONG-TERM ATTACHMENT

Love manifests in different forms and stages, from the intense and often irrational feelings of infatuation to the deep, enduring bond of long-term attachment. Each stage of love is characterized by unique neurological processes and hormonal changes that shape our emotions and behaviors. This chapter explores the science behind infatuation and long-term attachment, providing insights into how the brain and body respond to different phases of romantic relationships.

Infatuation: The Initial Rush

Infatuation, often described as "falling in love," is the first stage of romantic love. It is characterized by intense emotions, heightened energy, and a focus on the beloved that can border on obsession. This stage is driven by a complex interplay of neurotransmitters and hormones that create feelings of euphoria and excitement associated with new love.

Neurological Basis of Infatuation:

The brain's reward system plays a crucial role in infatuation. Key regions involved include the ventral tegmental area (VTA), the nucleus accumbens, and the caudate nucleus. These areas are rich in dopamine, a neurotransmitter associated with pleasure and reward.

- Dopamine: During infatuation, the brain releases high levels of dopamine in response to stimuli related to the loved one. This surge in dopamine creates feelings of euphoria, increased energy, and heightened focus on the partner. Dopamine also reinforces behaviors that bring us closer to our loved ones, motivating us to seek their company and maintain the relationship.

- Norepinephrine: Another neurotransmitter, norepinephrine, is involved in the physical symptoms of infatuation, such as increased heart rate, sweating, and a sense of exhilaration. Norepinephrine enhances alertness and arousal, contributing to the intense emotions experienced during this stage.

- Serotonin: Interestingly, serotonin levels decrease during infatuation, similar to those observed in individuals with obsessive-compulsive disorder (OCD). This decrease can lead to obsessive thoughts about the loved one and a preoccupation with the relationship.

Hormonal Changes:

Infatuation also triggers changes in hormone levels that influence our emotions and behaviors.

- Testosterone and Estrogen: Both men and women experience fluctuations in sex hormones during infatuation. Testosterone, which increases libido and assertiveness, rises in women, while estrogen, which enhances nurturing behaviors, rises in men. These hormonal changes support the pursuit and formation of romantic relationships.

- Oxytocin: Known as the "love hormone," oxytocin is released during physical touch, such as hugging, kissing, and sexual activity. Oxytocin promotes bonding and trust, reinforcing the emotional connection between partners.

Behavioral Effects:

The neurological and hormonal changes during infatuation lead to distinct behavioral patterns.

- Increased Energy and Focus: Individuals in the infatuation stage often experience a burst of energy and heightened focus on their partner. They may have difficulty concentrating on other tasks and spend considerable time thinking about their loved ones.

- Risk-Taking and Novelty-Seeking: Infatuation can increase willingness to take risks and seek out new experiences, driven by the desire to impress and bond with the partner. This behavior is linked to the dopamine surge in the brain's reward system.

- Idealization: Infatuated individuals tend to idealize their partners, focusing on their positive traits and overlooking flaws. This idealization can create an unrealistic perception of the loved one, which may need to be adjusted as the relationship progresses.

Long-Term Attachment: The Enduring Bond

As the initial intensity of infatuation wanes, romantic relationships often transition to a phase of long-term attachment. This stage is characterized by deep emotional bonds, mutual support, and stability. The neurological and hormonal processes involved in long-term attachment differ from those in infatuation, reflecting the shift from passionate love to companionate love.

Neurological Basis of Long-Term Attachment:

The brain regions and neurotransmitters involved in long-term attachment support emotional bonding, trust, and commitment.

- Oxytocin and Vasopressin: Oxytocin continues to play a crucial role in long-term attachment, promoting feelings of closeness and trust. Vasopressin, another hormone associated with social bonding, complements the effects of oxytocin. Together, these hormones reinforce the emotional bond and encourage monogamous behaviors.

- Endorphins: Endorphins, the body's natural painkillers, are released during physical affection and shared positive experiences. They create a sense of well-being and emotional security, contributing to the stability of long-term relationships.

- Prefrontal Cortex: Unlike the reduced activity in the prefrontal cortex during infatuation, this region becomes more active in long-term attachment. The prefrontal cortex supports rational decision-making, impulse control, and emotional regulation, helping partners navigate the complexities of a long-term relationship.

Hormonal Changes:

Long-term attachment involves hormonal changes that support emotional stability and commitment.

- Reduced Dopamine Levels: While dopamine levels are still involved in maintaining attraction, they decrease from the intense levels seen during infatuation. This reduction reflects the transition from the high excitement of new love to the more stable satisfaction of long-term attachment.

- Stable Serotonin Levels: Serotonin levels normalize during long-term attachment, supporting emotional balance and reducing the obsessive thinking characteristic of infatuation.

Behavioral Effects:

The shift to long-term attachment brings about changes in behavior that promote relationship stability and satisfaction.

- Emotional Bonding: Partners in long-term relationships experience deep emotional bonding, characterized by mutual support, trust, and intimacy. This bonding is reinforced by regular physical affection, shared experiences, and effective communication.

- Commitment and Monogamy: Long-term attachment often involves a commitment to monogamy and mutual support. The release of oxytocin and vasopressin strengthens this commitment, encouraging partners to invest in the relationship and work through challenges together.

- Conflict Resolution: The increased activity in the prefrontal cortex during long-term attachment supports better conflict resolution and emotional regulation. Partners are more likely to approach conflicts constructively, seeking solutions that strengthen the relationship rather than escalate tensions.

The Transition from Infatuation to Long-Term Attachment

The transition from infatuation to long-term attachment is a natural progression in romantic relationships, but it can also be a challenging period. Understanding the neurological and hormonal changes involved can help partners navigate this transition more effectively.

Adjusting Expectations:

As the initial intensity of infatuation fades, partners may need to adjust their expectations of the relationship. Recognizing that the passionate feelings of early love are likely to evolve into a deeper, more stable bond can help manage this transition.

Fostering Emotional Intimacy:

Maintaining emotional intimacy is crucial for long-term attachment. Regular physical affection, open communication, and shared experiences can strengthen the emotional bond and promote relationship satisfaction.

Navigating Challenges:

The transition from infatuation to long-term attachment can bring challenges, such as reduced novelty and increased familiarity. Partners can address these challenges by seeking out new experiences together, maintaining individual interests, and prioritizing the relationship.

Building Trust and Commitment:

Trust and commitment are foundational to long-term attachment. Partners can build trust by being reliable, honest, and supportive. Commitment involves a mutual dedication to the relationship and a willingness to work through difficulties together.

Conclusion

The science behind infatuation and long-term attachment reveals the intricate neurological and hormonal processes that shape our romantic relationships. While infatuation is characterized by intense emotions and heightened energy driven by dopamine and other neurotransmitters, long-term attachment involves deep emotional bonding supported by oxytocin, vasopressin, and endorphins.

Understanding these processes provides valuable insights into the different stages of love and the natural progression of romantic relationships. By recognizing the unique characteristics and challenges of each stage, individuals can navigate their relationships with greater awareness and intentionality, fostering lasting love and fulfillment.

As we continue to explore the science of love, we gain a deeper appreciation for the complex interplay between the brain, body, and emotions in shaping our most profound human experiences. This knowledge empowers us to build healthier, more satisfying relationships, enhancing our overall well-being and happiness.

CASE STUDIES AND BRAIN IMAGING STUDIES ON LOVE

The study of love has evolved significantly with advancements in neuroscience and technology, particularly through the use of brain imaging techniques. These tools have provided profound insights into the neurological processes underlying romantic love, infatuation, and long-term attachment. This chapter explores key case studies and brain imaging research that shed light on how love manifests in the brain.

Brain Imaging Techniques in the Study of Love

Before diving into specific case studies, it's essential to understand the primary brain imaging techniques used in this research.

Functional Magnetic Resonance Imaging (fMRI):

fMRI measures brain activity by detecting changes in blood flow. When a brain region is more active, it consumes more oxygen, leading to increased blood flow to that area. This technique is non-invasive and provides high-resolution images of brain activity in real time, making it ideal for studying the dynamic processes involved in love.

Positron Emission Tomography (PET):

PET scans measure metabolic activity in the brain by detecting radioactive tracers injected into the bloodstream. This technique helps researchers observe how different brain regions use glucose and other substances, providing insights into the brain's functioning during various emotional states.

Electroencephalography (EEG):

EEG measures electrical activity in the brain using electrodes placed on the scalp. While it offers less spatial resolution than fMRI or PET, EEG provides excellent temporal resolution, capturing rapid changes in brain activity associated with different emotional and cognitive states.

Case Studies on Infatuation and Romantic Love

Helen Fisher's fMRI Studies on Early-Stage Romantic Love:

Helen Fisher, a leading anthropologist and researcher in the study of love, conducted groundbreaking fMRI studies to investigate the neural correlates of early-stage romantic love.

- Study Design: Fisher's team recruited individuals who reported being deeply in love within the past six months. Participants were shown pictures of their romantic partners, as well as neutral images, while undergoing fMRI scans.

- Findings: The scans revealed significant activation in the ventral tegmental area (VTA) and the caudate nucleus, both regions rich in dopamine receptors. These areas are associated with the brain's reward and motivation systems, explaining the feelings of euphoria and obsession often experienced in early love. The research also showed reduced activity in brain regions associated with critical thinking and social judgment, such as the prefrontal cortex, suggesting that love can lead to idealized perceptions of the partner.

Arthur Aron's Study on Love and the Brain:

Psychologist Arthur Aron conducted pioneering research using fMRI to explore the neural basis of romantic love.

- Study Design: Aron's study involved participants who were in long-term romantic relationships. They were shown photographs of their partners while undergoing fMRI scans.

- Findings: The scans revealed that long-term romantic love activates brain regions associated with reward, motivation, and attachment, similar to those activated in early-stage love. Notably, the ventral pallidum, a region linked to long-term bonding and attachment, showed significant activation. This finding suggests that the brain maintains certain mechanisms of romantic love over the long term, supporting the stability and satisfaction of enduring relationships.

Brain Imaging Studies on Long-Term Attachment

Bianca Acevedo's Research on Long-Term Love:

Bianca Acevedo, a researcher specializing in love and attachment, used fMRI to study the neural correlates of long-term romantic love.

- Study Design: Acevedo's study involved participants who reported being in long-term, loving relationships for over 20 years. Participants were shown pictures of their partners and other familiar individuals while undergoing fMRI scans.

- Findings: The scans showed that long-term romantic love activates brain regions associated with attachment, such as the ventral pallidum and the posterior hippocampus. These areas are involved in social bonding and memory, highlighting the importance of emotional connection and shared experiences in sustaining long-term love. The study also found continued activation of the brain's reward system, suggesting that long-term partners still evoke feelings of pleasure and reward.

The Role of Oxytocin and Vasopressin:

Numerous studies have highlighted the roles of oxytocin and vasopressin in long-term attachment. These hormones are crucial for social bonding and pair-bond formation.

- Oxytocin Research: fMRI studies have shown that oxytocin release during physical affection and positive social interactions enhances activity in brain regions associated with trust and bonding. For example, a study by Ruth Feldman found that couples who engaged in more affectionate touch had higher levels of oxytocin and stronger activation in the anterior cingulate cortex, a region linked to empathy and social connection.

- Vasopressin Research: Vasopressin is another hormone linked to long-term attachment. Research by Larry Young has demonstrated that vasopressin influences the formation of pair bonds in both animals and humans. fMRI studies indicate that vasopressin receptor-rich areas, such as the ventral pallidum, show increased activity during long-term romantic attachment, underscoring the hormone's role in maintaining monogamous relationships.

The Impact of Love on Mental Health

Love and Stress Reduction:

Research has shown that romantic love and long-term attachment can positively impact mental health by reducing stress and promoting emotional well-being.

- Study by Lisa Diamond: Lisa Diamond's research demonstrated that physical affection with a romantic partner reduces cortisol levels, a hormone associated with stress. Participants who received hugs or engaged in intimate conversations with their partners showed significant reductions in cortisol, indicating that romantic relationships can serve as a buffer against stress.

- Emotional Regulation: Long-term romantic relationships enhance emotional regulation by providing emotional support and stability. Brain imaging studies have shown that individuals in stable relationships have greater activity in the prefrontal cortex, which is involved in regulating emotions and managing stress. This finding suggests that the emotional support provided by a romantic partner can enhance mental resilience and overall well-being.

Case Studies on Love and Social Bonding

The Role of Social Support in Romantic Relationships:

Romantic relationships often serve as a primary source of social support, which is crucial for emotional and psychological health.

- Study by Brooke Feeney: Brooke Feeney's research explored the impact of social support in romantic relationships. Participants who reported high levels of perceived support from their partners showed greater activation in brain regions associated with reward and positive emotions, such as the nucleus accumbens and the anterior insula. These findings highlight the importance of social support in enhancing relationship satisfaction and individual well-being.

Love and Empathy:

Romantic love enhances empathy and compassion towards the partner, fostering deeper emotional connections.

- Study by Tania Singer: Tania Singer conducted fMRI studies to investigate the neural basis of empathy in romantic relationships. Participants were scanned while observing their partners experiencing pain. The scans revealed significant activation in brain regions associated with empathy, such as the anterior insula and the anterior cingulate cortex. This research underscores the role of empathy in strengthening romantic bonds and promoting emotional intimacy.

Conclusion

Brain imaging studies and case research have significantly advanced our understanding of the neurological processes underlying romantic love and long-term attachment. These studies highlight the critical roles of neurotransmitters, hormones, and specific brain regions in shaping our experiences of love, infatuation, and enduring bonds.

By exploring the neural correlates of love, researchers have provided valuable insights into how romantic relationships influence our emotions, behaviors, and overall well-being. This knowledge enhances our appreciation for the complex interplay between the brain and love, offering a deeper understanding of one of humanity's most profound and universal experiences.

As we continue to investigate the science of love, we can apply these insights to foster healthier, more fulfilling relationships. Understanding the neurological basis of love empowers us to navigate the complexities of romance with greater awareness and intentionality, ultimately enhancing our capacity for deep and lasting connections.

CHAPTER 05

SEXUAL ATTRACTION

Evolutionary Theories of Sexual Attraction

Sexual attraction is a fundamental aspect of human behavior, deeply rooted in our evolutionary history. Understanding the evolutionary theories of sexual attraction provides valuable insights into why certain traits are universally appealing and how these preferences have shaped human mating strategies over millennia. This chapter explores key evolutionary concepts and theories that explain the dynamics of sexual attraction.

The Foundations of Evolutionary Theory

Evolutionary theory, primarily based on the work of Charles Darwin, posits that traits and behaviors that enhance an organism's chances of survival and reproduction are more likely to be passed on to future generations. This process, known as natural selection, drives the evolution of species over time.

Sexual Selection:

Sexual selection is a specific type of natural selection that focuses on traits that increase an individual's chances of attracting mates and successfully reproducing. Darwin identified two main mechanisms of sexual selection:

1. Intrasexual Competition: Competition among members of the same sex for access to mates. Typically, this involves males competing with other males for the attention of females.

2. Intersexual Selection: Preference by one sex for certain traits in members of the opposite sex. Typically, this involves females selecting males based on traits they find attractive.

Key Evolutionary Theories of Sexual Attraction

Parental Investment Theory:

Parental investment theory, proposed by Robert Trivers, suggests that the sex that invests more in offspring (typically females) will be more selective in choosing mates, while the sex that invests less (typically males) will compete more intensely for access to mates. This theory explains many observed differences in male and female mating behaviors.

- Female Selectivity: Females typically invest more in offspring through pregnancy, childbirth, and nurturing. As a result, they are more selective in choosing mates, prioritizing traits that indicate good genes, resource availability, and the ability to provide parental care.

- Male Competition: Males, with lower direct investment in offspring, compete for access to females. Traits that enhance their competitive edge, such as physical strength, dominance, and resource acquisition, are favored.

Good Genes Hypothesis:

The good genes hypothesis suggests that individuals select mates based on traits that signal genetic quality and health, ensuring that their offspring inherit beneficial genes. These traits often include physical attractiveness, symmetry, and indicators of health.

- Physical Attractiveness: Traits such as facial symmetry, clear skin, and physical fitness are seen as indicators of good genes and overall health. These traits are universally considered attractive because they suggest an individual's ability to produce healthy offspring.

- Symmetry and Health: Symmetrical features are thought to indicate developmental stability and genetic robustness. Studies have shown that people with more symmetrical faces and bodies are often perceived as more attractive and are more successful in attracting mates.

Handicap Principle:

Proposed by Amotz Zahavi, the handicap principle suggests that certain traits that appear to be costly or disadvantageous can actually serve as honest signals of genetic quality. These traits indicate that an individual can afford to bear the costs, suggesting superior genetics.

- Costly Signals: Examples of costly signals include peacocks' elaborate tails, which are energetically expensive to produce and maintain. In humans, traits such as bravery, risk-taking, and displays of wealth can serve as costly signals that attract mates.

Mate Choice and Sexual Dimorphism:

Sexual dimorphism refers to differences in appearance and behavior between males and females of a species. In humans, these differences are influenced by sexual selection and reflect the different strategies and preferences of each sex.

- Male Traits: Traits such as facial hair, broad shoulders, and deep voices are influenced by testosterone and signal masculinity and reproductive fitness. These traits are often attractive to females, especially during ovulation when preferences for masculine features peak.

- Female Traits: Traits such as a low waist-to-hip ratio, full lips, and high-pitched voices are influenced by estrogen and signal fertility and health. These traits are often attractive to males, who prioritize indicators of reproductive potential.

Evolutionary Psychology and Human Mating Strategies

Evolutionary psychology applies principles of evolutionary theory to understand the psychological mechanisms that underpin human behavior, including mating strategies.

Short-Term and Long-Term Mating Strategies:

Humans employ both short-term and long-term mating strategies, influenced by evolutionary pressures and individual circumstances.

Short-Term Mating: Short-term mating strategies focus on maximizing reproductive opportunities with multiple partners. Traits that enhance short-term mating success include physical attractiveness, social dominance, and willingness to engage in casual sex. Men are generally more inclined towards short-term mating due to their ability to father many offspring with minimal investment.

- Long-Term Mating: Long-term mating strategies prioritize forming stable, enduring relationships that support offspring survival and development. Traits that enhance long-term mating success include resource provision, emotional stability, and willingness to invest in the relationship and offspring. Women are generally more inclined towards long-term mating due to their significant investment in offspring.

Mate Preferences and Trade-Offs:

Individuals often face trade-offs in mate selection, balancing different traits based on their priorities and circumstances.

- Good Genes vs. Good Provider: Women may face a trade-off between selecting a mate with good genes (physical attractiveness, genetic health) and a good provider (resource availability, reliability). This trade-off can influence mating strategies and preferences, especially under different environmental conditions.

- Short-Term Attractiveness vs. Long-Term Compatibility: Men may face a trade-off between selecting a mate who is highly attractive for short-term mating and one who offers long-term compatibility and mutual investment. Balancing these preferences can impact relationship dynamics and satisfaction.

Mate Copying:

Mate copying refers to the tendency to be influenced by the mate choices of others. This phenomenon can enhance an individual's chances of selecting a high-quality mate by relying on social information and the preferences of peers.

- Social Proof: Observing others' mate choices provides social proof that a potential partner possesses desirable traits. This can increase the attractiveness of individuals who are seen as successful in attracting mates, creating a feedback loop that enhances their desirability.

- Cultural and Social Influences: Mate copying is influenced by cultural and social factors, such as peer groups, media representations, and societal norms. These influences can shape individual preferences and mating behaviors, reflecting broader patterns of attraction within a community.

Evolutionary Perspectives on Modern Mating Behaviors

While evolutionary theories provide a foundational understanding of sexual attraction, modern social and cultural contexts also play a significant role in shaping mating behaviors.

Online Dating and Technology:

The rise of online dating and technology-mediated communication has transformed mating behaviors, offering new opportunities and challenges for mate selection.

- Increased Options: Online dating platforms provide access to a larger pool of potential mates, increasing opportunities for both short-term and long-term relationships. This can amplify evolutionary tendencies, such as prioritizing physical attractiveness and initial impressions.

- Presentation and Selection: The way individuals present themselves online, through photos and profiles, reflects and reinforces evolutionary preferences. People often emphasize traits that signal genetic quality, resource availability, and social status to attract potential mates.

Cultural Evolution and Mating Preferences:

Cultural evolution, the process by which cultural practices and norms change over time, influences mating preferences and behaviors.

- Changing Norms: Societal norms around gender roles, marriage, and family structure continue to evolve, impacting mate selection strategies. For example, increasing gender equality and changing economic conditions can shift priorities in mate preferences, emphasizing traits like mutual support and shared values.

- Cross-Cultural Variability: Mating preferences and behaviors vary across cultures, reflecting different environmental and social pressures. Understanding these cultural differences provides a more nuanced view of sexual attraction and highlights the interplay between biological and cultural factors.

Conclusion

Evolutionary theories of sexual attraction offer a comprehensive framework for understanding the deep-seated preferences and behaviors that shape human mating strategies. From parental investment and good genes hypotheses to sexual dimorphism and mate copying, these theories explain why certain traits are universally appealing and how they contribute to reproductive success.

While evolutionary principles provide a foundational understanding, modern social and cultural contexts also play a crucial role in shaping mating behaviors. The interplay between biology and culture creates a dynamic landscape of attraction, reflecting the complexity and diversity of human relationships.

By integrating insights from evolutionary theory with an understanding of contemporary influences, we can gain a deeper appreciation for the forces that drive sexual attraction and mate selection. This knowledge enhances our ability to navigate the complexities of romantic relationships, fostering healthier and more fulfilling connections.

DIFFERENCES IN ATTRACTION BETWEEN GENDERS

Sexual attraction manifests differently in men and women due to a combination of biological, psychological, and sociocultural factors. These differences can be traced back to evolutionary pressures that have shaped distinct mating strategies and preferences for each gender. Understanding these differences provides insight into how and why men and women are attracted to certain traits and behaviors in potential mates.

Evolutionary Basis for Gender Differences

From an evolutionary perspective, the distinct reproductive roles of men and women have led to differing priorities and strategies in mate selection. These differences are rooted in the need to maximize reproductive success and ensure the survival of offspring.

Parental Investment Theory:

According to parental investment theory, proposed by Robert Trivers, the sex that invests more in offspring (typically females) will be more selective in choosing mates, while the sex that invests less (typically males) will compete more intensely for access to mates.

- Female Selectivity: Women typically invest more in reproduction through pregnancy, childbirth, and child-rearing. As a result, they are more selective in their mate choices, prioritizing traits that signal resource availability, stability, and genetic fitness.

- Male Competition: Men, with lower direct investment in offspring, tend to compete more for mating opportunities. This competition has led to the evolution of traits and behaviors that enhance their attractiveness and ability to secure mates.

Key Differences in Attraction

Physical Attractiveness:

Both men and women value physical attractiveness, but the specific traits considered attractive often differ between genders due to evolutionary pressures.

- Men's Preferences: Men are generally attracted to physical traits that signal fertility and reproductive health. These traits include a youthful appearance, clear skin, and a low waist-to-hip ratio. Studies have shown that men prefer women with a waist-to-hip ratio of approximately 0.7, which is associated with higher fertility and lower risk of disease.

- Women's Preferences: Women are attracted to physical traits that signal genetic quality, health, and the ability to provide protection and resources. Traits such as broad shoulders, a strong jawline, and facial symmetry are often considered attractive. During ovulation, women's preferences for more masculine features and behaviors intensify, suggesting a heightened sensitivity to indicators of genetic fitness during peak fertility.

Resource Provision and Social Status:

Women place a higher value on a potential mate's ability to provide resources and social status, reflecting the evolutionary need for support during pregnancy and child-rearing.

- Resource Provision: Women often prefer men who demonstrate the ability to provide resources, such as financial stability, ambition, and industriousness. These traits suggest that the man can support a family and ensure the survival of offspring.

- Social Status: Social status is another critical factor in women's attraction to men. Higher social status is associated with greater access to resources and protection, making high-status men more attractive as potential mates. Indicators of social status include professional success, education, and social influence.

Emotional and Social Traits:

While physical and resource-related traits are important, emotional and social traits also play a significant role in attraction for both genders.

- Men's Preferences: Men often value traits that suggest warmth, kindness, and nurturing ability in women.

These traits indicate a potential partner's capability to care for children and create a supportive home environment.

- Women's Preferences: Women prioritize emotional stability, kindness, and the ability to form strong social bonds in potential mates. These traits suggest that a man will be a reliable partner and a supportive co-parent. Women also value traits that enhance emotional intimacy and communication, as these contribute to relationship stability and satisfaction.

Sexual Strategies and Short-Term vs. Long-Term Mating:

Men and women exhibit different preferences and behaviors when it comes to short-term and long-term mating strategies, influenced by their reproductive roles and investment levels.

- Short-Term Mating: Men are generally more open to short-term mating opportunities and place a higher emphasis on physical attractiveness and sexual availability in these contexts. This preference aligns with the evolutionary strategy of maximizing reproductive opportunities with minimal investment.

- Long-Term Mating: Women are more selective in short-term mating contexts due to the potential costs associated with pregnancy and the need for support. In long-term mating, both men and women prioritize traits that enhance relationship stability and parental investment, such as emotional compatibility, commitment, and mutual support.

Psychological and Sociocultural Influences

In addition to evolutionary factors, psychological and sociocultural influences play a significant role in shaping attraction and mate preferences.

Psychological Factors:

Individual experiences, personality traits, and psychological needs can influence attraction in both men and women.

- Attachment Styles: Attachment theory suggests that early relationships with caregivers shape adult romantic relationships. Securely attached individuals tend to form healthy, stable relationships, while those with anxious or avoidant attachment styles may face challenges in attraction and relationship maintenance.

- Personality Traits: Traits such as openness, conscientiousness, and agreeableness can influence attraction and relationship satisfaction. People often seek partners with compatible or complementary personality traits.

Sociocultural Factors:

Cultural norms, societal expectations, and socialization processes also impact gender differences in attraction.

- Cultural Norms: Cultural norms dictate what is considered attractive and acceptable in potential mates. These norms can vary widely across societies, influencing preferences for traits such as physical appearance, social status, and gender roles.

- Media and Socialization: Media representations of ideal beauty and successful relationships shape individual preferences and expectations. Socialization processes, including family upbringing and peer interactions, reinforce these ideals and influence attraction.

Changing Gender Roles:

Shifts in gender roles and increased gender equality have influenced attraction and mate preferences in modern society.

- Evolving Preferences: As gender roles become more fluid, preferences for traditional traits such as resource provision and physical attractiveness may evolve. For example, women in modern societies with greater gender equality may place less emphasis on a man's financial status and more on shared responsibilities and emotional support.

- Mutual Support: Modern relationships often emphasize mutual support and shared responsibilities, reflecting a shift towards more egalitarian partnerships. This shift influences attraction by prioritizing traits that enhance collaboration and equal partnership.

Conclusion

Gender differences in attraction are shaped by a combination of evolutionary, psychological, and sociocultural factors. While evolutionary theories provide a foundational understanding of why men and women prioritize certain traits, psychological and sociocultural influences add complexity and variability to these preferences.

Understanding these differences helps illuminate the diverse and multifaceted nature of human attraction. By recognizing the interplay of biology, psychology, and culture, individuals can navigate their romantic relationships with greater awareness and adaptability, fostering healthier and more fulfilling connections.

As society continues to evolve, so too will the dynamics of attraction, reflecting ongoing changes in gender roles, cultural norms, and individual experiences. Embracing this complexity enriches our understanding of human relationships and enhances our ability to form meaningful and lasting bonds.

CULTURAL INFLUENCES ON SEXUAL ATTRACTION

Sexual attraction is not solely driven by biological and psychological factors; it is also profoundly shaped by cultural influences. Culture encompasses the beliefs, norms, values, and practices shared by a group of people, and it plays a crucial role in determining what is considered attractive and desirable. This chapter explores how different cultures influence sexual attraction, examining the diverse ways in which cultural contexts shape individual preferences and behaviors.

The Role of Culture in Shaping Attraction

Culture influences sexual attraction in several key ways, including through societal norms, media representations, and cultural practices. These influences can vary widely across different societies, leading to diverse standards of beauty and attractiveness.

Societal Norms and Values:

Societal norms and values dictate what is considered attractive within a particular culture. These norms are often reinforced through socialization processes, including family upbringing, education, and peer interactions.

- Beauty Standards: Different cultures have varying standards of beauty that influence what traits are considered attractive. For example, in some cultures, a fuller body figure is associated with health and prosperity, while in others, a slimmer physique is idealized. These standards can impact individual preferences and perceptions of attractiveness.

- Gender Roles: Cultural norms around gender roles also influence attraction. In societies with traditional gender roles, traits that align with these roles—such as masculinity and assertiveness in men, and femininity and nurturing qualities in women—are often considered attractive. In more egalitarian societies, attraction may be based on traits that support equality and partnership.

Media Representations:

Media plays a significant role in shaping perceptions of attractiveness by portraying certain traits and behaviors as desirable. Television, movies, magazines, and social media all contribute to creating and perpetuating cultural ideals of beauty and attractiveness.

- Celebrity Influence: Celebrities often embody cultural ideals of attractiveness and serve as role models for desirable traits. Their appearances and behaviors set trends that influence public perceptions and individual preferences.

- Advertising and Marketing: Advertisements frequently use attractive models to promote products, reinforcing cultural standards of beauty. These representations can impact how individuals perceive their own attractiveness and the attractiveness of others.

Cultural Practices and Traditions:

Cultural practices and traditions also shape sexual attraction by dictating the rituals and behaviors associated with courtship and mate selection.

- Courtship Rituals: Different cultures have unique courtship rituals that influence how attraction is expressed and pursued. For example, in some cultures, arranged marriages are common, and attraction may develop after marriage. In others, dating and romantic relationships before marriage are the norm, with attraction playing a central role in mate selection.

- Beauty Practices: Cultural practices related to beauty and grooming can influence attraction. For instance, practices such as body modification, makeup, and clothing styles reflect cultural ideals and enhance perceived attractiveness. These practices vary widely across cultures, reflecting different standards and preferences.

Cross-Cultural Differences in Attraction

Examining cross-cultural differences in attraction reveals the diverse ways in which culture shapes preferences and behaviors. These differences highlight the influence of cultural context on what individuals find attractive and desirable.

Western vs. Non-Western Standards of Beauty:

Western cultures often emphasize traits such as slimness, youthfulness, and facial symmetry as standards of beauty. These traits are frequently promoted through media and fashion industries.

- Slimness: In many Western cultures, a slim physique is considered attractive and associated with health and fitness. This standard is reinforced by media representations and societal pressures, leading individuals to prioritize physical fitness and diet.

- Youthfulness: Youthful features, such as smooth skin and a lack of wrinkles, are highly valued in Western cultures. The emphasis on youthfulness is often linked to perceptions of fertility and vitality.

- Facial Symmetry: Symmetrical facial features are considered attractive in many Western societies, as they are associated with genetic health and developmental stability.

In contrast, non-Western cultures may have different standards of beauty that reflect their unique cultural values and environmental conditions.

- Fuller Body Figures: In some non-Western cultures, fuller body figures are considered attractive and signify health, wealth, and fertility. This preference can be seen in parts of Africa and the Pacific Islands, where larger body sizes are associated with prosperity and social status.

- Traditional Dress and Adornments: Non-Western cultures often emphasize traditional dress and adornments as markers of beauty and attractiveness. For example, the use of colorful fabrics, intricate jewelry, and body art can enhance perceived attractiveness and reflect cultural heritage.

Cultural Variability in Gender Roles and Attraction:

Gender roles and expectations vary across cultures, influencing what traits are considered attractive in men and women.

- Masculinity and Femininity: In cultures with traditional gender roles, traits associated with masculinity (such as strength, dominance, and assertiveness) are often valued in men, while traits associated with femininity (such as nurturing, empathy, and submissiveness) are valued in women. These preferences reinforce gender norms and expectations.

- Egalitarian Societies: In more egalitarian societies, attraction may be based on traits that support equality and partnership, such as mutual respect, shared responsibilities, and emotional compatibility. These societies may prioritize traits like kindness, intelligence, and sense of humor over traditional gendered traits.

The Influence of Globalization on Attraction

Globalization has led to increased cultural exchange and the blending of different cultural standards of attractiveness. This phenomenon has both homogenizing and diversifying effects on attraction.

Homogenization of Beauty Standards:

Globalization has contributed to the spread of Western beauty standards worldwide, often leading to a homogenization of attractiveness ideals.

- Media Influence: The global reach of Western media, including Hollywood movies, television shows, and fashion magazines, promotes Western beauty standards and influences perceptions of attractiveness in non-Western cultures.

- Cosmetic Industry: The global cosmetic industry reinforces Western beauty ideals by marketing products that emphasize slimness, youthfulness, and facial symmetry. This influence can lead to the adoption of Western beauty practices in non-Western cultures.

Cultural Hybridization:

At the same time, globalization has led to cultural hybridization, where different cultural standards of beauty and attraction merge to create new, diverse ideals.

- Fusion of Traditions: Cultural hybridization can result in the fusion of traditional and modern beauty practices, creating unique standards of attractiveness that incorporate elements from multiple cultures. For example, contemporary fashion in many countries blends traditional attire with Western styles.

- Celebration of Diversity: Increased cultural exchange can promote the celebration of diverse beauty standards and challenge narrow definitions of attractiveness. This can lead to greater acceptance and appreciation of different body types, skin tones, and facial features.

Sociocultural Movements and Changing Standards

Sociocultural movements and changes in societal values also play a role in shaping standards of attraction and challenging traditional norms.

Body Positivity Movement:

The body positivity movement advocates for the acceptance of all body types and challenges narrow beauty standards that prioritize slimness and youthfulness.

- Diverse Representation: The movement promotes diverse representation in media and advertising, encouraging the inclusion of individuals with different body shapes, sizes, and abilities. This representation helps expand the definition of attractiveness and fosters greater self-acceptance.

- Empowerment: By challenging unrealistic beauty standards, the body positivity movement empowers individuals to embrace their natural appearance and focus on overall well-being rather than conforming to societal pressures.

Gender Equality and Attraction:

Advancements in gender equality and changing gender roles influence attraction by shifting priorities and preferences.

- Shared Responsibilities: As gender roles become more fluid and egalitarian, traits that support shared responsibilities and mutual respect become more important in attraction. This shift reflects a growing emphasis on partnership and collaboration in relationships.

- Valuing Non-Traditional Traits: Gender equality promotes the valuation of non-traditional traits, such as emotional intelligence and caregiving abilities in men, and ambition and independence in women. These changes challenge traditional gender norms and broaden the range of traits considered attractive.

Conclusion

Cultural influences play a significant role in shaping sexual attraction, reflecting the diverse values, norms, and practices of different societies. From societal norms and media representations to cultural practices and globalization, these influences create a rich tapestry of standards and preferences that vary widely across cultures.

Understanding the impact of culture on attraction highlights the importance of context in shaping individual preferences and behaviors. It also underscores the dynamic nature of attraction, as cultural norms and values continue to evolve in response to social and technological changes.

By appreciating the cultural dimensions of attraction, we can develop a more nuanced understanding of human relationships and foster greater acceptance of diverse standards of beauty and desirability. This knowledge enhances our ability to navigate the complexities of attraction with cultural sensitivity and respect, ultimately enriching our connections with others.

CHAPTER 06

CHEMISTRY IN RELATIONSHIPS

How Attraction Evolves into Love and Commitment

The journey from initial attraction to enduring love and commitment is a complex process influenced by biological, psychological, and social factors. This chapter explores how the initial spark of attraction evolves into deeper emotional bonds, leading to long-term commitment and partnership. Understanding these stages provides insight into the dynamics of romantic relationships and the elements that contribute to their success.

The Stages of Romantic Relationships

Romantic relationships typically progress through several stages, each characterized by distinct emotions, behaviors, and neurological processes. These stages include initial attraction, infatuation, deepening intimacy, and long-term commitment.

Initial Attraction:

Initial attraction is driven by physical appearance, personality traits, and situational factors. This stage involves a combination of biological and psychological processes that create the first spark of interest between individuals.

- Physical Attraction: Physical appearance plays a significant role in initial attraction, with traits such as facial symmetry, body shape, and grooming influencing perceptions of attractiveness.

- Personality and Behavior: Personality traits such as confidence, humor, and kindness can enhance initial attraction. Positive interactions and social skills also contribute to creating a favorable first impression.

- Situational Factors: Context and environment influence initial attraction. Proximity, shared activities, and social settings can facilitate opportunities for interaction and increase the likelihood of attraction.

Infatuation:

Infatuation, often referred to as "falling in love," is characterized by intense emotions, heightened arousal, and a focus on the beloved. This stage is driven by a surge of neurotransmitters and hormones that create feelings of euphoria and obsession.

- Neurochemical Changes: During infatuation, the brain releases high levels of dopamine, norepinephrine, and serotonin, creating feelings of excitement, energy, and preoccupation with the partner.

- Behavioral Effects: Infatuated individuals may display behaviors such as increased attention to the partner, frequent communication, and a desire to spend as much time together as possible. Idealization of the partner and overlooking flaws are common during this stage.

Deepening Intimacy:

As infatuation begins to stabilize, relationships enter a phase of deepening intimacy. This stage involves building emotional connections, trust, and mutual understanding.

- Emotional Bonding: Emotional intimacy develops through sharing personal experiences, vulnerabilities, and feelings. This process fosters a deeper connection and strengthens the bond between partners.

- Trust and Reliability: Trust is established through consistent and reliable behavior, open communication, and mutual support. Trust enhances emotional security and reduces anxiety in the relationship.

- Shared Experiences: Engaging in shared activities and creating positive memories together contribute to deepening intimacy. These experiences build a sense of partnership and mutual investment in the relationship.

Long-Term Commitment:

Long-term commitment represents the culmination of the relationship's evolution, characterized by a stable, enduring bond and a commitment to maintaining the partnership over time.

- Attachment and Bonding: Long-term commitment is supported by the release of oxytocin and vasopressin, hormones that promote attachment and bonding. These hormones reinforce the emotional connection and enhance relationship stability.

- Mutual Support and Dependability: Committed partners provide mutual support and dependability, fostering a sense of security and partnership. They work together to navigate challenges and maintain the relationship.

- Shared Goals and Values: Long-term commitment involves aligning goals, values, and life plans. Partners who share similar aspirations and values are more likely to sustain a fulfilling and harmonious relationship.

The Role of Communication in Relationship Evolution

Effective communication is crucial in navigating the stages of relationship evolution. It facilitates understanding, resolves conflicts, and strengthens emotional bonds.

Open and Honest Communication:

Open and honest communication builds trust and ensures that both partners feel heard and understood.

- Expressing Feelings and Needs: Partners should express their feelings, needs, and concerns openly and respectfully. This practice fosters emotional intimacy and helps address issues before they escalate.

- Active Listening: Active listening involves paying full attention to the partner, acknowledging their perspective, and responding thoughtfully. It demonstrates empathy and validates the partner's experiences.

Conflict Resolution:

Conflicts are inevitable in relationships, but how they are managed can determine the relationship's success.

- Constructive Conflict Resolution: Constructive conflict resolution involves addressing disagreements calmly and respectfully, seeking solutions rather than blaming. This approach helps resolve issues while preserving the relationship's integrity.

- Compromise and Negotiation: Compromise and negotiation are essential in finding mutually acceptable solutions. Partners should be willing to make concessions and find common ground.

Factors Influencing Relationship Success

Several factors influence the success and longevity of romantic relationships, including compatibility, emotional intelligence, and external support.

Compatibility:

Compatibility in values, interests, and life goals enhances relationship satisfaction and stability.

- Values and Beliefs: Shared values and beliefs create a strong foundation for a relationship. Partners who align in their core principles are more likely to navigate life challenges harmoniously.

- Interests and Activities: Shared interests and activities provide opportunities for bonding and enjoyment. Engaging in common hobbies and pursuits strengthens the connection between partners.

Emotional Intelligence:

Emotional intelligence, the ability to understand and manage one's emotions and those of others, is critical for relationship success.

- Self-Awareness: Self-awareness involves recognizing and understanding one's emotions and how they affect behavior. It enables individuals to respond to relationship dynamics thoughtfully.

- Empathy and Understanding: Empathy involves understanding and sharing the feelings of the partner. It fosters compassion and helps address emotional needs effectively.

- Emotion Regulation: Emotion regulation is the ability to manage and respond to emotions constructively. It helps maintain stability and reduces the impact of negative emotions on the relationship.

External Support:

External support from family, friends, and social networks can positively impact relationship success.

- Social Support: Social support provides emotional and practical assistance, enhancing relationship resilience. Supportive social networks can help couples navigate challenges and celebrate successes.

- Relationship Counseling: Professional counseling and therapy can provide valuable tools and strategies for managing relationship issues. Counseling can help partners improve communication, resolve conflicts, and strengthen their bond.

Challenges in Maintaining Long-Term Relationships

While long-term relationships offer numerous benefits, they also present challenges that require effort and commitment to overcome.

Routine and Monotony:

Routine and monotony can diminish excitement and novelty in long-term relationships.

- Maintaining Novelty: Maintaining novelty involves introducing new activities, experiences, and challenges to keep the relationship dynamic. Regularly exploring new interests together can reignite excitement and passion.

- Spontaneity and Surprise: Spontaneity and surprise can add excitement and unpredictability to the relationship. Small gestures, surprises, and spontaneous adventures can strengthen the emotional connection.

External Stressors:

External stressors, such as work pressures, financial challenges, and family responsibilities, can strain relationships.

- Stress Management: Effective stress management involves developing strategies to cope with external pressures. Partners should support each other in managing stress and prioritize self-care.

- Work-Life Balance: Balancing work and personal life is crucial for maintaining relationship health. Partners should allocate quality time for each other and ensure that work demands do not overshadow the relationship.

Communication Breakdown:

Communication breakdowns can lead to misunderstandings and unresolved conflicts.

- Regular Check-Ins: Regular check-ins involve setting aside time to discuss the relationship, share feelings, and address any concerns. These conversations help maintain open lines of communication and prevent issues from festering.

- Repairing Communication: Repairing communication involves addressing and resolving breakdowns promptly. Partners should practice active listening, empathy, and patience in rebuilding effective communication.

Conclusion

The evolution of attraction into love and commitment is a multifaceted process influenced by biological, psychological, and social factors. Understanding the stages of romantic relationships and the elements that contribute to their success provides valuable insights into maintaining healthy and fulfilling partnerships.

Effective communication, compatibility, emotional intelligence, and external support are critical factors in fostering long-term commitment and relationship satisfaction. By navigating challenges with empathy, understanding, and mutual effort, couples can build strong, enduring bonds that enhance their well-being and happiness.

As we continue to explore the science of relationships, we gain a deeper appreciation for the complexities and dynamics of love. This knowledge empowers individuals to cultivate meaningful connections and navigate the journey from attraction to commitment with greater awareness and intentionality.

COMMUNICATION AND EMOTIONAL INTIMACY IN RELATIONSHIPS

Communication and emotional intimacy are foundational elements of healthy and fulfilling romantic relationships. They enable partners to connect on a deep emotional level, fostering trust, understanding, and mutual support. This chapter explores the importance of communication and emotional intimacy in relationships, examining how they contribute to relationship satisfaction and stability.

The Role of Communication in Relationships

Effective communication is essential for building and maintaining healthy relationships. It allows partners to express their needs, desires, and concerns, fostering mutual understanding and cooperation.

Types of Communication:

1. Verbal Communication:

- Expressing Thoughts and Feelings: Verbal communication involves sharing thoughts, feelings, and experiences with a partner. This exchange of information helps partners understand each other's perspectives and emotions.

- Active Listening: Active listening involves paying full attention to the speaker, acknowledging their message, and responding thoughtfully. It demonstrates empathy and validation, reinforcing the emotional connection between partners.

2. Nonverbal Communication:

- Body Language: Nonverbal cues such as facial expressions, gestures, and posture convey emotions and intentions. Positive body language, such as eye contact and smiling, enhances emotional intimacy.

- Touch and Physical Affection: Physical touch, such as hugging, holding hands, and cuddling, communicates love and affection. It releases oxytocin, the "love hormone," promoting bonding and emotional closeness.

3. Digital Communication:

- Texting and Messaging: Digital communication through texting and messaging allows partners to stay connected throughout the day. It provides opportunities for sharing quick updates, expressing affection, and maintaining emotional connection.

- Video Calls and Social Media: Video calls enable face-to-face interaction when partners are physically apart, helping maintain intimacy. Social media can also serve as a platform for expressing love and celebrating the relationship publicly.

Effective Communication Skills:

1. Clarity and Honesty:

- Being Clear and Direct: Clear and direct communication minimizes misunderstandings and ensures that both partners understand each other's messages. Avoiding vague language and being specific about needs and desires enhances clarity.

- Honesty and Transparency: Honesty is crucial for building trust and emotional intimacy. Being open and transparent about feelings, intentions, and concerns fosters a sense of security and authenticity in the relationship.

2. Empathy and Understanding:

- Practicing Empathy: Empathy involves understanding and sharing the feelings of a partner. It requires putting oneself in the partner's shoes and responding with compassion and support.

- Validation: Validation means acknowledging and accepting a partner's feelings and experiences, even if they differ from one's own. It demonstrates respect and reinforces emotional connection.

3. Conflict Resolution:

- Constructive Conflict Resolution: Constructive conflict resolution involves addressing disagreements calmly and respectfully, seeking solutions rather than assigning blame. It helps resolve issues while preserving the relationship's integrity.

- Compromise and Negotiation: Compromise and negotiation are essential for finding mutually acceptable solutions. Partners should be willing to make concessions and find common ground.

The Importance of Emotional Intimacy

Emotional intimacy refers to the deep emotional connection and closeness between partners. It involves sharing vulnerabilities, fears, and dreams, creating a sense of mutual trust and understanding.

Building Emotional Intimacy:

1. Vulnerability and Trust:

- Sharing Vulnerabilities: Sharing vulnerabilities involves opening up about fears, insecurities, and past experiences. It fosters emotional closeness and helps partners understand each other's inner world.

- Building Trust: Trust is built through consistent and reliable behavior, honesty, and emotional support. It creates a safe space for partners to express themselves without fear of judgment or rejection.

2. Quality Time and Shared Experiences:

- Spending Quality Time Together: Quality time involves engaging in meaningful activities that strengthen the emotional bond. It can include shared hobbies, date nights, and intimate conversations.

- Creating Positive Memories: Shared experiences and positive memories enhance emotional intimacy. Celebrating milestones, going on adventures, and creating traditions build a sense of partnership and connection.

3. Emotional Support and Validation:

- Providing Emotional Support: Emotional support involves being there for a partner during difficult times, offering comfort, encouragement, and understanding. It reinforces the emotional bond and fosters a sense of security.

- Validating Feelings: Validation means acknowledging and accepting a partner's feelings without judgment. It demonstrates empathy and reinforces the partner's emotional experience.

Challenges to Emotional Intimacy:

1. Fear of Vulnerability:

- Overcoming Fear of Vulnerability: Fear of vulnerability can hinder emotional intimacy. Partners should work on building trust and creating a safe space for open expression.

- Addressing Past Trauma: Past trauma can impact the ability to be vulnerable. Seeking therapy and support can help individuals heal and build healthier emotional connections.

2. Communication Barriers:

- Identifying Communication Barriers: Communication barriers such as misunderstandings, assumptions, and defensiveness can impede emotional intimacy. Identifying and addressing these barriers is crucial for improving communication.

- Improving Communication Skills: Partners should work on enhancing their communication skills, including active listening, empathy, and clarity. Practicing effective communication fosters emotional intimacy.

3. External Stressors:

- Managing External Stressors: External stressors such as work pressures, financial challenges, and family responsibilities can strain emotional intimacy. Partners should support each other in managing stress and prioritize self-care.

- Maintaining Work-Life Balance: Balancing work and personal life is essential for maintaining emotional intimacy. Allocating quality time for the relationship helps strengthen the emotional bond.

The Role of Emotional Intelligence

Emotional intelligence, the ability to understand and manage one's emotions and those of others, is crucial for fostering communication and emotional intimacy in relationships.

Components of Emotional Intelligence:

1. Self-Awareness:

- Recognizing Emotions: Self-awareness involves recognizing and understanding one's emotions and how they impact behavior. It enables individuals to respond thoughtfully to relationship dynamics.

- Reflecting on Experiences: Reflecting on experiences helps individuals gain insights into their emotional responses and patterns. It promotes personal growth and enhances emotional intimacy.

2. Self-Regulation:

- Managing Emotions: Self-regulation involves managing and responding to emotions constructively. It helps maintain stability and reduces the impact of negative emotions on the relationship.

- Practicing Patience and Resilience: Practicing patience and resilience enhances emotional regulation. It enables individuals to navigate challenges calmly and effectively.

3. Empathy:

- Understanding Partner's Emotions: Empathy involves understanding and sharing the feelings of a partner. It fosters compassion and helps address emotional needs effectively.

- Responding with Compassion: Responding with compassion involves offering support and understanding to a partner in distress. It reinforces the emotional connection and strengthens the relationship.

4. Social Skills:

- Effective Communication: Social skills include effective communication, conflict resolution, and relationship management. They enhance emotional intimacy and foster healthy interactions.

- Building Positive Relationships: Building positive relationships involves nurturing connections through empathy, support, and mutual respect. It creates a supportive and fulfilling relational environment.

Strategies for Enhancing Communication and Emotional Intimacy

Several strategies can help couples enhance communication and emotional intimacy in their relationships.

Regular Check-Ins:

- Scheduling Regular Check-Ins: Regular check-ins involve setting aside time to discuss the relationship, share feelings, and address any concerns. These conversations help maintain open lines of communication and prevent issues from festering.

- Creating a Safe Space: Creating a safe space for check-ins involves approaching conversations with empathy, openness, and non-judgment. It ensures that both partners feel heard and understood.

Emotional Expression:

- Expressing Gratitude and Appreciation: Regularly expressing gratitude and appreciation for a partner's efforts and qualities enhances emotional intimacy. It reinforces positive behaviors and strengthens the emotional bond.

- Sharing Dreams and Aspirations: Sharing dreams and aspirations fosters emotional intimacy by creating a sense of partnership and mutual support. It helps partners understand each other's long-term goals and aspirations.

Conflict Resolution Techniques:

- Using "I" Statements: Using "I" statements instead of "you" statements reduces defensiveness and promotes constructive communication. It focuses on expressing personal feelings and needs rather than blaming the partner.

- Seeking Compromise: Seeking compromise involves finding mutually acceptable solutions to conflicts. It requires flexibility, empathy, and a willingness to make concessions.

Enhancing Physical Intimacy:

- Maintaining Physical Affection: Regular physical affection, such as hugging, kissing, and cuddling, enhances emotional intimacy. It releases oxytocin, promoting bonding and emotional closeness.

- Prioritizing Sexual Intimacy: Prioritizing sexual intimacy involves maintaining a healthy and satisfying sexual relationship. It enhances emotional connection and reinforces the physical bond.

Conclusion

Communication and emotional intimacy are vital components of healthy and fulfilling romantic relationships. They enable partners to connect on a deep emotional level, fostering trust, understanding, and mutual support.

Effective communication involves clarity, honesty, empathy, and constructive conflict resolution. Emotional intimacy is built through vulnerability, trust, shared experiences, and emotional support. Together, they create a strong foundation for long-term commitment and relationship satisfaction.

By enhancing communication skills, nurturing emotional intimacy, and addressing challenges with empathy and understanding, couples can build strong, enduring bonds that enhance their well-being and happiness. As we continue to explore the dynamics of relationships, we gain a deeper appreciation for the importance of communication and emotional intimacy in fostering meaningful and fulfilling connections.

CONFLICT RESOLUTION AND THE CHEMISTRY OF FORGIVENESS

Conflict is an inevitable part of any relationship, but how couples manage and resolve conflicts can significantly impact the health and longevity of their relationship. Effective conflict resolution fosters understanding, strengthens the bond between partners, and promotes a healthier, more resilient relationship. Additionally, the ability to forgive and move past conflicts plays a crucial role in maintaining emotional intimacy and trust. This chapter explores the importance of conflict resolution and forgiveness, examining the underlying psychological and biochemical processes that facilitate these essential relational skills.

The Nature of Conflict in Relationships

Conflict arises from differences in needs, desires, values, and perceptions. While conflict is natural, unresolved disputes can lead to stress, resentment, and deterioration of the relationship.

Sources of Conflict:

1. Communication Issues: Misunderstandings, poor communication, and lack of clarity can lead to conflicts. Effective communication is key to preventing and resolving misunderstandings.

2. Differences in Values and Beliefs: Conflicts often arise from differing values, beliefs, and priorities. Respecting and understanding these differences is crucial for conflict resolution.

3. Power and Control: Struggles over power, control, and decision-making can create tension. Balancing power dynamics is essential for a healthy relationship.

4. Financial Stress: Money-related issues, such as budgeting, spending, and saving, can be significant sources of

conflict. Open discussions about finances can help mitigate these conflicts.

5. Intimacy and Sexual Issues: Differences in sexual needs and desires, as well as issues related to emotional intimacy, can lead to conflicts. Addressing these topics openly and sensitively is important.

Conflict Resolution Strategies

Effective conflict resolution involves a combination of communication skills, empathy, and problem-solving techniques. Here are some key strategies for resolving conflicts constructively:

Active Listening:

Active listening involves fully concentrating on the speaker, understanding their message, and responding thoughtfully. This practice demonstrates empathy and validation, fostering a supportive environment for conflict resolution.

- Reflective Listening: Reflective listening involves paraphrasing the speaker's message to ensure understanding. It shows that you are attentive and genuinely interested in their perspective.

- Nonverbal Cues: Maintaining eye contact, nodding, and using appropriate facial expressions convey attentiveness and empathy.

Using "I" Statements:

"I" statements focus on expressing personal feelings and needs without blaming the partner. This approach reduces defensiveness and promotes constructive dialogue.

- Example: Instead of saying, "You never listen to me," say, "I feel unheard when I don't get a chance to express my thoughts."

Identifying Underlying Issues:

Conflicts often stem from deeper issues rather than immediate disagreement. Identifying and addressing these underlying issues is crucial for lasting resolution.

- Root Cause Analysis: Discussing the root causes of conflicts helps partners understand each other's perspectives and work towards meaningful solutions.

Seeking Compromise:

Compromise involves finding mutually acceptable solutions that address the needs and concerns of both partners. It requires flexibility, empathy, and a willingness to make concessions.

- Win-Win Solutions: Aim for solutions that benefit both partners and strengthen the relationship.

Setting Boundaries:

Setting boundaries helps prevent conflicts from escalating and ensures respectful interactions.

- Establishing Rules: Agreeing on ground rules for conflict resolution, such as no yelling or name-calling, creates a safe and constructive environment for addressing issues.

Time-Outs:

Taking a time-out allows partners to cool down and reflect before continuing the discussion. This strategy can prevent conflicts from escalating and promote rational problem-solving.

- Calm Reflection: Use the time-out to calm down, gather thoughts, and approach the conflict with a clearer mind.

Mediation and Counseling:

Seeking the help of a mediator or relationship counselor can provide valuable tools and strategies for resolving conflicts. Professional guidance can help couples navigate difficult issues and improve their conflict resolution skills.

- Professional Support: Therapists and counselors offer neutral perspectives and effective techniques for managing conflicts.

The Chemistry of Forgiveness

Forgiveness is a vital component of healthy relationships, enabling partners to move past conflicts and rebuild trust. The process of forgiveness involves both psychological and biochemical mechanisms that promote healing and emotional intimacy.

Psychological Aspects of Forgiveness:

1. Empathy and Understanding:

Empathy involves understanding and sharing the feelings of the partner who has caused hurt. It fosters compassion and facilitates the forgiveness process.

- Perspective-Taking: Seeing the situation from the partner's perspective helps in understanding their motivations and reducing negative emotions.

2. Letting Go of Resentment:

Forgiveness involves letting go of resentment, anger, and the desire for retribution. It requires a conscious decision to move past the hurt and focus on healing.

- Emotional Release: Allowing oneself to feel and release negative emotions is crucial for genuine forgiveness.

3. Rebuilding Trust:

Rebuilding trust is a gradual process that requires consistent and reliable behavior, honesty, and open communication.

- Consistent Actions: Demonstrating trustworthy behavior over time helps in restoring trust and strengthening the relationship.

Biochemical Aspects of Forgiveness:

1. Oxytocin:

Oxytocin, often referred to as the "love hormone," plays a significant role in bonding and emotional intimacy. It is released during physical touch and positive social interactions, promoting feelings of trust and connection.

- Physical Affection: Engaging in physical affection, such as hugging and cuddling, releases oxytocin and enhances emotional closeness.

2. Endorphins:

Endorphins are natural painkillers that create feelings of well-being and reduce stress. Positive interactions and acts of forgiveness can trigger the release of endorphins, promoting emotional healing.

- Positive Activities: Engaging in enjoyable activities together can boost endorphin levels and strengthen the emotional bond.

3. Cortisol Reduction:

Cortisol is a stress hormone that is elevated during conflicts and negative emotions. Forgiveness and positive interactions can lower cortisol levels, reducing stress and promoting emotional well-being.

- Stress Management: Practicing relaxation techniques, such as deep breathing and mindfulness, can help reduce cortisol levels and support the forgiveness process.

The Process of Forgiveness

Forgiveness is a complex process that involves several stages, each requiring effort and commitment from both partners.

Stages of Forgiveness:

1. Acknowledgment:

Acknowledging the hurt and its impact on the relationship is the first step in the forgiveness process. Both partners need to recognize the issue and its emotional consequences.

- Open Discussion: Discussing the hurt openly and honestly helps in understanding each other's feelings and perspectives.

2. Expression of Remorse:

The partner who caused the hurt should express genuine remorse and take responsibility for their actions. This expression demonstrates a commitment to making amends.

- Sincere Apology: Offering a sincere apology and acknowledging the impact of the actions fosters emotional healing.

3. Decision to Forgive:

Forgiveness involves a conscious decision to let go of negative emotions and move towards healing. It requires a willingness to work through the hurt and rebuild trust.

- Commitment to Forgive: Making a firm commitment to forgive helps in focusing on positive actions and emotional recovery.

4. Rebuilding Trust:

Rebuilding trust is a gradual process that requires consistent and reliable behavior, open communication, and mutual support.

- Trust-Building Actions: Engaging in trust-building actions, such as keeping promises and demonstrating honesty, reinforces the commitment to the relationship.

5. Healing and Moving Forward:

The final stage of forgiveness involves emotional healing and moving forward together. It requires a focus on positive interactions, shared experiences, and mutual growth.

- Positive Reinforcement: Reinforcing positive behaviors and celebrating progress helps in strengthening the emotional bond and promoting relationship satisfaction.

The Benefits of Forgiveness

Forgiveness offers numerous benefits for both individual well-being and relationship health.

Individual Benefits:

1. Emotional Healing:

Forgiveness promotes emotional healing by reducing negative emotions and fostering a sense of peace and closure.

- Reduced Stress: Letting go of resentment and anger lowers stress levels and enhances emotional well-being.

2. Improved Mental Health:

Forgiveness is associated with improved mental health outcomes, including reduced symptoms of depression, anxiety, and PTSD.

- Positive Mental State: Practicing forgiveness enhances overall mental health and contributes to a positive outlook on life.

Relationship Benefits:

1. Strengthened Bond:

Forgiveness strengthens the emotional bond between partners by promoting trust, empathy, and mutual support.

- Enhanced Intimacy: Forgiveness fosters emotional intimacy and deepens the connection between partners.

2. Increased Relationship Satisfaction:

Relationships characterized by forgiveness and effective conflict resolution tend to have higher levels of satisfaction and stability.

- Long-Term Commitment: Forgiveness contributes to long-term commitment and relationship resilience.

Conclusion

Conflict resolution and the chemistry of forgiveness are vital components of healthy and fulfilling relationships. Effective conflict resolution involves active listening, empathy, and problem-solving skills, while forgiveness requires emotional understanding, letting go of resentment, and rebuilding trust.

The psychological and biochemical processes underlying forgiveness promote emotional healing, reduce stress, and enhance relationship satisfaction. By mastering conflict resolution and practicing forgiveness, couples can navigate challenges, strengthen their bond, and build a resilient and enduring partnership.

As we continue to explore the dynamics of relationships, we gain a deeper appreciation for the importance of these skills in fostering meaningful and fulfilling connections. This knowledge empowers individuals to cultivate healthier, more supportive relationships, ultimately enhancing their well-being and happiness.

CHAPTER 07

ATTRACTION ACROSS THE LIFESPAN

Attraction and Love in Adolescence

Adolescence is a critical period of development characterized by significant physical, emotional, and social changes. During this time, individuals begin to experience attraction and love in new and profound ways. Understanding how attraction and love manifest in adolescence provides valuable insights into the developmental processes that shape romantic relationships throughout life. This chapter explores the nature of attraction and love in adolescence, examining the biological, psychological, and social factors that influence young people's romantic experiences.

Biological Changes and Adolescent Attraction

The onset of puberty marks the beginning of adolescence and brings about a series of biological changes that significantly impact attraction and romantic behavior.

Hormonal Changes:

During puberty, the body undergoes hormonal changes that stimulate the development of secondary sexual characteristics and increase sexual desire.

- Testosterone and Estrogen: The production of testosterone in boys and estrogen in girls increases during puberty, leading to physical changes such as the development of facial and body hair, breast development, and changes in body shape. These hormones also play a crucial role in the development of sexual attraction and desire.

- Sexual Maturation: As adolescents become sexually mature, they start to experience sexual feelings and fantasies. These changes heighten their interest in romantic relationships and increase their focus on physical attractiveness and sexual compatibility.

Brain Development:

The adolescent brain undergoes significant development, particularly in areas related to emotion regulation, decision-making, and social behavior.

- Prefrontal Cortex: The prefrontal cortex, responsible for decision-making and impulse control, continues to develop during adolescence. This development helps adolescents navigate complex social situations and make more informed choices in their romantic relationships.

- Limbic System: The limbic system, which includes structures such as the amygdala and hippocampus, is involved in processing emotions and rewards. During adolescence, increased activity in the limbic system contributes to heightened emotional responses and the intensity of romantic feelings.

Psychological Factors and Adolescent Love

Psychological factors play a significant role in shaping how adolescents experience attraction and love. These factors include identity formation, emotional development, and cognitive changes.

Identity Formation:

Adolescence is a time of self-discovery and identity formation. As adolescents explore their personal values, beliefs, and goals, their experiences with attraction and love contribute to their understanding of who they are and what they seek in relationships.

- Exploration and Experimentation: Adolescents often engage in exploration and experimentation in their romantic relationships. They may date different people, experience varying levels of intimacy, and navigate the complexities of romantic attachment.

- Self-Concept: Romantic experiences during adolescence influence self-concept and self-esteem. Positive relationships can enhance self-confidence, while negative experiences can lead to self-doubt and insecurity.

Emotional Development:

Emotional development during adolescence involves learning to manage and express emotions in healthy ways. Romantic relationships provide opportunities for emotional growth and the development of emotional intelligence.

- Intense Emotions: Adolescents often experience intense emotions in their romantic relationships, including joy, excitement, jealousy, and heartbreak. These emotions are amplified by hormonal changes and the developmental stage of the brain.

- Emotional Regulation: Learning to regulate emotions is a critical aspect of adolescent development. Successful emotional regulation in romantic relationships involves managing feelings of jealousy, anger, and disappointment, as well as expressing love and affection.

Cognitive Changes:

Cognitive development during adolescence enhances the ability to think abstractly, consider multiple perspectives, and understand complex social dynamics.

- Perspective-Taking: Adolescents develop the ability to take the perspective of others, which is essential for empathy and understanding in romantic relationships. This skill helps them navigate conflicts and build deeper connections with their partners.

- Future Orientation: As adolescents mature, they begin to consider the long-term implications of their romantic choices. This future orientation influences their decisions about commitment, exclusivity, and sexual activity.

Social Influences on Adolescent Attraction

Social influences, including peer relationships, family dynamics, and cultural norms, play a crucial role in shaping adolescent attraction and romantic behavior.

Peer Relationships:

Peers are a significant source of influence during adolescence, impacting attitudes, behaviors, and preferences related to attraction and love.

- Social Comparison: Adolescents often compare themselves to their peers in terms of romantic experiences and attractiveness. This social comparison can influence self-esteem and relationship choices.

- Peer Pressure: Peer pressure can affect romantic behavior, including the timing of first relationships, levels of intimacy, and choices about sexual activity. Adolescents may feel pressure to conform to peer norms and expectations.

Family Dynamics:

Family relationships and parenting styles also influence adolescent romantic behavior and attitudes towards love.

- Parental Support: Supportive and open communication with parents can provide adolescents with guidance and reassurance in their romantic relationships. Parental involvement can help adolescents navigate challenges and make informed decisions.

- Family Models: Adolescents often model their romantic behavior on the relationships they observe within their family. Positive role models can promote healthy relationship behaviors, while negative models may lead to dysfunctional patterns.

Cultural Norms:

Cultural norms and societal expectations shape attitudes towards attraction, dating, and romantic relationships in adolescence.

- Dating Practices: Cultural norms dictate acceptable behaviors and practices in dating, such as the appropriate age to start dating, the roles of males and females, and expectations around intimacy and commitment.

- Media Influence: Media representations of romance and attraction influence adolescent perceptions of love and relationships. Television shows, movies, music, and social media often portray idealized and sometimes unrealistic views of romantic relationships.

Challenges and Opportunities in Adolescent Relationships

Adolescent romantic relationships present both challenges and opportunities for growth and development. Understanding these dynamics can help adolescents navigate their romantic experiences more effectively.

Challenges:

1. Emotional Vulnerability: Adolescents are emotionally vulnerable and may experience intense feelings of love and heartbreak. Managing these emotions can be challenging and requires support and guidance.

2. Peer Pressure: Navigating peer pressure and social expectations can complicate romantic relationships. Adolescents may struggle to balance their desires with the need to fit in with their peer group.

3. Risky Behaviors: Romantic relationships can sometimes lead to risky behaviors, such as early sexual

activity, substance use, and unsafe practices. Educating adolescents about safe and healthy relationship behaviors is crucial.

Opportunities:

1. Emotional Growth: Romantic relationships provide opportunities for emotional growth, including the development of empathy, emotional regulation, and communication skills.

2. Identity Formation: Romantic experiences contribute to identity formation and self-discovery. Adolescents learn about their values, preferences, and what they seek in a partner.

3. Social Skills: Navigating romantic relationships helps adolescents develop essential social skills, such as conflict resolution, negotiation, and collaboration.

Supporting Healthy Adolescent Relationships

Supporting adolescents in developing healthy romantic relationships involves providing education, guidance, and resources. Parents, educators, and mentors play a crucial role in this process.

Education and Communication:

1. Comprehensive Relationship Education: Providing adolescents with comprehensive education about relationships, including topics such as communication,

consent, emotional intelligence, and conflict resolution, equips them with the knowledge and skills needed for healthy relationships.

2. Open Communication: Encouraging open communication between adolescents and trusted adults fosters a supportive environment for discussing romantic experiences and seeking advice. Adolescents should feel comfortable discussing their feelings and concerns without fear of judgment.

Promoting Positive Role Models:

1. Positive Role Models: Highlighting positive relationship role models in the media, community, and family can inspire adolescents to develop healthy relationship behaviors. Role models can demonstrate respect, empathy, and mutual support.

2. Mentorship Programs: Mentorship programs that pair adolescents with older peers or adults can provide guidance and support in navigating romantic relationships. Mentors can offer valuable insights and advice based on their experiences.

Addressing Risks and Challenges:

1. Risk Awareness: Educating adolescents about the risks associated with romantic relationships, including sexual

health, consent, and emotional well-being, empowers them to make informed decisions.

2. Support Services: Providing access to support services, such as counseling and health services, ensures that adolescents have the resources they need to address relationship challenges and seek help when needed.

Conclusion

Attraction and love in adolescence are influenced by a complex interplay of biological, psychological, and social factors. Understanding these influences provides valuable insights into the developmental processes that shape romantic relationships during this critical period of life.

By supporting adolescents in developing healthy relationship behaviors, we can help them navigate the challenges and opportunities of romantic relationships. Education, open communication, positive role models, and access to support services are essential components of fostering healthy and fulfilling relationships in adolescence.

As we continue to explore the dynamics of attraction and love across the lifespan, we gain a deeper appreciation for the importance of nurturing healthy relationships from a young age. This knowledge empowers individuals to build strong, supportive, and resilient connections throughout their lives, enhancing their overall well-being and happiness.

MIDDLE-AGED LOVE: CHALLENGES AND REWARDS

Middle age, typically defined as the period between the mid-30s and mid-50s, is a time of significant life transitions and evolving personal and relational dynamics. During this stage, individuals often face unique challenges and experience new rewards in their romantic relationships. Understanding the complexities of middle-aged love provides valuable insights into how relationships evolve and adapt over time. This chapter explores the challenges and rewards of love in middle age, examining the factors that influence romantic relationships and the strategies for maintaining a fulfilling partnership.

Challenges of Middle-Aged Love

Middle age brings about various challenges that can impact romantic relationships. These challenges often stem from changes in personal circumstances, health, career, and family dynamics.

Life Transitions:

Middle age is often marked by significant life transitions that can affect romantic relationships.

1. Career Changes:

- Professional Stress: Middle-aged individuals may experience career-related stress, including job changes, promotions, or job loss. These changes can impact the time and energy available for maintaining a relationship.

- Work-Life Balance: Balancing work responsibilities with personal life becomes increasingly important. Striking a healthy balance is crucial for sustaining a romantic relationship.

2. Family Responsibilities:

- Parenting Demands: For many, middle age coincides with raising children, which can place significant demands on time and emotional resources. Parenting challenges, such as managing teenagers or preparing for children to leave home, can strain relationships.

- Caring for Aging Parents: The responsibility of caring for aging parents can add stress and reduce the time available for a partner. Navigating these dual caregiving roles requires careful coordination and support.

Health and Aging:

Physical and emotional health changes during middle age can influence romantic relationships.

1. Health Issues:

- Chronic Conditions: The onset of chronic health conditions, such as diabetes, heart disease, or arthritis, can impact the quality of life and the dynamics of a relationship.

- Physical Changes: Natural aging processes, such as changes in metabolism, energy levels, and physical appearance, can affect self-esteem and body image, influencing romantic and sexual relationships.

2. Mental and Emotional Health:

- Emotional Well-being: Middle age can bring about emotional challenges, including stress, anxiety, and midlife crises. These emotional fluctuations can impact relationship satisfaction and stability.

- Intimacy and Desire: Changes in sexual desire and intimacy levels can occur during middle age, requiring partners to communicate openly and adapt to evolving needs.

Relationship Dynamics:

The dynamics of a romantic relationship can evolve during middle age, presenting both challenges and opportunities.

1. Communication Issues:

- Communication Breakdown: Long-term relationships may experience communication breakdowns, where partners become less effective at expressing their needs and listening to each other.

- Conflict Resolution: Unresolved conflicts and recurring issues can accumulate over time, leading to resentment and dissatisfaction.

2. Emotional Distance:

- Growing Apart: Some couples may experience emotional distance as their interests and priorities diverge over time. Maintaining emotional closeness requires effort and intentionality.

- Rekindling Romance: Keeping the romantic spark alive can be challenging amid the routines and responsibilities of middle age. Couples need to find ways to rekindle and sustain romance.

Rewards of Middle-Aged Love

Despite the challenges, middle-aged love offers unique rewards and opportunities for growth, deepening connection, and mutual fulfillment.

Emotional Maturity:

Middle-aged individuals often bring greater emotional maturity to their relationships, enhancing their ability to navigate challenges and build deeper connections.

1. Self-Awareness:

- Personal Growth: Middle-aged individuals typically have a clearer understanding of themselves, their values, and their goals. This self-awareness contributes to more authentic and fulfilling relationships.

- Emotional Regulation: With age often comes improved emotional regulation, enabling individuals to manage conflicts constructively and maintain emotional stability.

2. Empathy and Understanding:

- Deeper Connection: Emotional maturity enhances empathy and understanding, allowing partners to connect on a deeper emotional level. This connection fosters trust and intimacy.

- Supportive Partnership: Middle-aged couples are often better equipped to provide mutual support and navigate life's challenges together.

Stability and Commitment:

Long-term relationships during middle age benefit from increased stability and commitment, providing a solid foundation for continued growth and satisfaction.

1. Shared History:

- Common Experiences: Couples who have been together for many years share a rich history of experiences, memories, and accomplishments. This shared history strengthens the bond and creates a sense of continuity.

- Overcoming Challenges: Having navigated previous challenges together, middle-aged couples often have a stronger sense of resilience and confidence in their relationship's ability to endure.

2. Mutual Investment:

- Commitment to Growth: Middle-aged couples are typically invested in each other's growth and well-being. This mutual investment fosters a sense of partnership and shared purpose.

- Future Planning: Couples in middle age often engage in future planning, including retirement and shared goals. This planning reinforces their commitment to a shared future.

Opportunities for Rediscovery:

Middle age can be a time of rediscovery and renewal in romantic relationships, offering opportunities to explore new interests and deepen the connection.

1. Empty Nest Syndrome:

- Renewed Focus on Partnership: As children leave home, couples have the opportunity to refocus on their partnership and explore new interests together. This transition can reinvigorate the relationship.

- Travel and Adventure: Many middle-aged couples take advantage of increased freedom to travel and engage in new adventures, creating shared memories and experiences.

2. Personal Development:

- Hobbies and Interests: Middle age provides the opportunity to pursue hobbies and interests that may have been set aside during earlier stages of life. Sharing these interests with a partner can strengthen the bond.

- Continued Learning: Engaging in continued learning and personal development can bring new dimensions to the relationship, fostering intellectual and emotional growth.

Strategies for Maintaining a Fulfilling Relationship

Maintaining a fulfilling romantic relationship during middle age requires intentional effort, effective communication, and mutual support. Here are some strategies to enhance relationship satisfaction and longevity:

Effective Communication:

1. Open Dialogue:

- Regular Check-Ins: Schedule regular check-ins to discuss the relationship, share feelings, and address concerns. These conversations help maintain open lines of communication and prevent issues from festering.

- Active Listening: Practice active listening by fully concentrating on the partner's message, acknowledging their perspective, and responding thoughtfully.

2. Conflict Resolution:

- Constructive Approach: Address conflicts constructively by focusing on solutions rather than blame. Use "I" statements to express feelings and needs without assigning fault.

- Seeking Compromise: Find mutually acceptable solutions through compromise and negotiation. Prioritize the relationship's well-being over winning an argument.

Emotional Intimacy:

1. Building Emotional Closeness:

- Sharing Vulnerabilities: Foster emotional closeness by sharing personal experiences, fears, and dreams. Being vulnerable with each other enhances trust and intimacy.

- Providing Support: Offer emotional support during difficult times, providing comfort, encouragement, and understanding.

2. Maintaining Romance:

- Regular Date Nights: Schedule regular date nights to spend quality time together and keep the romantic spark alive. Engage in activities that both partners enjoy.

- Spontaneity and Surprise: Introduce spontaneity and surprise into the relationship through small gestures, unexpected gifts, or spontaneous outings.

Mutual Growth:

1. Shared Goals:

- Future Planning: Engage in future planning by discussing long-term goals and aspirations. Collaborate on creating a shared vision for the future.

- Joint Projects: Take on joint projects, such as home improvement, volunteering, or starting a business. Working together towards common goals strengthens the partnership.

2. Personal Development:

- Individual Interests: Encourage each other to pursue individual interests and passions. Supporting personal growth enhances overall relationship satisfaction.

- Continued Learning: Engage in continued learning together, such as taking classes, attending workshops, or exploring new hobbies. Learning and growing together fosters intellectual and emotional connection.

Conclusion

Middle-aged love is characterized by unique challenges and rewards that reflect the evolving dynamics of romantic relationships. While middle age brings about significant life transitions, health changes, and relationship dynamics, it also offers opportunities for emotional growth, stability, and rediscovery.

By embracing effective communication, building emotional intimacy, and supporting mutual growth, middle-aged couples can navigate the complexities of this life stage and maintain a fulfilling partnership. Understanding the factors that influence middle-aged love provides valuable insights into sustaining healthy and resilient relationships throughout the lifespan.

As we continue to explore the dynamics of attraction and love across different life stages, we gain a deeper appreciation for the evolving nature of romantic relationships. This knowledge empowers individuals to cultivate meaningful and enduring connections, enhancing their overall well-being and happiness.

LOVE AND ATTRACTION IN OLDER ADULTS

Love and attraction are not confined to youth; they continue to play a significant role in the lives of older adults. As people age, their experiences, perspectives, and priorities evolve, influencing how they perceive and engage in romantic relationships. Understanding the dynamics of love and attraction in older adults provides valuable insights into the enduring nature of human connection and the unique challenges and rewards that come with aging. This chapter explores how love and attraction manifest in older adults, examining the biological, psychological, and social factors that shape romantic relationships in later life.

Biological Factors Influencing Love and Attraction

As individuals age, biological changes can impact their romantic relationships. These changes influence physical health, sexual function, and overall well-being.

Physical Health:

Physical health plays a crucial role in the romantic lives of older adults. Health conditions and changes in physical capabilities can affect relationship dynamics and intimacy.

1. Chronic Illnesses:

- Impact on Intimacy: Chronic illnesses such as arthritis, diabetes, and cardiovascular diseases can impact physical intimacy and sexual activity. Managing these conditions and communicating openly with partners about limitations and needs is essential.

- Support and Caregiving: Health issues may require one partner to take on a caregiving role, which can alter the dynamics of the relationship. Providing support and maintaining emotional connection despite health challenges is crucial.

2. Energy Levels and Mobility:

- Adjusting Activities: Changes in energy levels and mobility may require adjustments in shared activities and routines. Finding new ways to spend quality time together can help maintain the bond.

Sexual Function:

Sexual function and desire may change with age, but many older adults continue to experience sexual satisfaction and intimacy.

1. Hormonal Changes:

- Menopause and Andropause: Hormonal changes such as menopause in women and andropause in men can affect sexual desire and function. Understanding and addressing these changes through medical intervention or lifestyle adjustments can help maintain sexual health.

- Libido and Desire: While libido may decrease for some, many older adults continue to experience a strong desire for intimacy. Open communication with partners about sexual needs and preferences is important.

2. Adaptations and Communication:

- Exploring Alternatives: Older adults may need to explore alternative forms of intimacy and sexual expression that accommodate physical changes. This exploration can enhance emotional closeness and satisfaction.

- Open Dialogue: Maintaining an open dialogue about sexual health and intimacy helps partners navigate changes together and find mutually satisfying solutions.

Psychological Factors Influencing Love and Attraction

Psychological well-being and emotional maturity significantly influence romantic relationships in older adults. These factors shape how individuals perceive love and attraction and how they navigate relationship dynamics.

Emotional Maturity:

Older adults often bring greater emotional maturity and life experience to their relationships, enhancing their ability to navigate challenges and build deep connections.

1. Self-Awareness:

- Understanding Needs: Older adults typically have a clearer understanding of their emotional needs and relationship preferences. This self-awareness helps them seek partners who align with their values and goals.

- Personal Growth: Life experiences contribute to personal growth and resilience, enabling older adults to handle relationship challenges with greater patience and wisdom.

2. Empathy and Compassion:

- Deeper Connection: Emotional maturity enhances empathy and compassion, allowing older adults to connect with their partners on a deeper emotional level. These qualities foster trust and intimacy.

- Supportive Partnership: Older adults often prioritize mutual support and companionship, creating a nurturing and stable relationship environment.

Life Satisfaction and Well-Being:

The overall well-being and life satisfaction of older adults influence their romantic relationships and ability to experience love and attraction.

1. Mental Health:

- Positive Outlook: Maintaining good mental health and a positive outlook on life contributes to relationship satisfaction. Older adults who engage in activities that promote mental well-being are better equipped to build fulfilling relationships.

- Addressing Challenges: Older adults may face mental health challenges such as depression or anxiety. Seeking support and treatment for these issues can improve overall well-being and relationship quality.

2. Life Purpose and Fulfillment:

- Shared Activities: Engaging in shared activities and pursuing common interests enhances life satisfaction and strengthens the bond between partners. Finding purpose and meaning together contributes to a fulfilling relationship.

- Continued Learning: Embracing opportunities for continued learning and personal development fosters intellectual and emotional growth, enriching the relationship.

Social Factors Influencing Love and Attraction

Social factors, including family dynamics, social networks, and cultural norms, play a significant role in shaping the romantic experiences of older adults.

Family Dynamics:

Family relationships and responsibilities can impact romantic relationships in later life.

1. Adult Children:

- Support and Involvement: Adult children may play a supportive role in their parents' romantic relationships, offering encouragement and acceptance. Positive family dynamics enhance relationship satisfaction.

- Boundaries and Independence: Maintaining healthy boundaries with adult children ensures that older adults can pursue their romantic relationships independently while still enjoying family support.

2. Grandparenting:

- Balancing Roles: Balancing the role of grandparent with a romantic relationship requires time and energy management. Involving a partner in grandparenting activities can create shared experiences and strengthen the bond.

Social Networks:

Social connections and community involvement influence the romantic lives of older adults.

1. Friendship and Support:

- Social Engagement: Maintaining an active social life and engaging with friends provides emotional support and reduces feelings of isolation. Social connections enhance overall well-being and relationship satisfaction.

- Community Involvement: Participating in community activities and groups offers opportunities to meet new people and form romantic connections.

2. Dating and Remarriage:

- Online Dating: Online dating platforms provide older adults with opportunities to meet potential partners, expanding their social networks and romantic prospects.

- Second Chances: Many older adults find love and companionship in remarriage or new long-term relationships. Embracing these opportunities with an open mind enhances life satisfaction.

Cultural Norms and Expectations:

Cultural attitudes towards aging and romance influence how older adults perceive and engage in romantic relationships.

1. Ageism and Stereotypes:

- Challenging Stereotypes: Challenging ageist stereotypes and promoting positive representations of older adults in romantic relationships helps combat societal biases and fosters acceptance.

- Cultural Norms: Different cultures have varying attitudes towards romance and aging. Understanding and respecting these norms can enhance relationship dynamics.

2. Changing Norms:

- Evolving Attitudes: Societal attitudes towards aging and romance are evolving, with increasing recognition of the importance of love and companionship in later life. Embracing these changes supports older adults in pursuing fulfilling relationships.

Rewards of Love and Attraction in Older Adults

Despite the challenges, love and attraction in older adults offer unique rewards and opportunities for deep connection, personal growth, and mutual fulfillment.

Emotional and Physical Intimacy:

1. Deep Emotional Connection:

- Shared Life Experience: Older adults bring a wealth of life experience to their relationships, enabling deep emotional connections and mutual understanding.

- Emotional Support: Providing and receiving emotional support fosters a sense of security and enhances overall well-being.

2. Physical Affection:

- Continued Intimacy: Many older adults continue to experience physical intimacy and affection, which promotes emotional closeness and relationship satisfaction.

- Adaptations and Creativity: Exploring new ways to express physical affection and intimacy can enhance connection and satisfaction.

Companionship and Partnership:

1. Mutual Support:

- Navigating Challenges: Older adults often prioritize mutual support, helping each other navigate health challenges, life transitions, and daily responsibilities.

- Shared Responsibilities: Collaborating on shared responsibilities and goals fosters a sense of partnership and teamwork.

2. Enjoyment and Fulfillment:

- Shared Activities: Engaging in enjoyable activities and shared interests enhances life satisfaction and strengthens the bond between partners.

- Purpose and Meaning: Finding purpose and meaning in the relationship contributes to overall fulfillment and happiness.

Opportunities for Growth and Rediscovery:

1. Personal Growth:

- Continued Learning: Embracing opportunities for continued learning and personal development enriches the relationship and fosters intellectual and emotional growth.

- Exploration and Adventure: Exploring new hobbies, interests, and experiences together brings excitement and novelty to the relationship.

2. Rediscovering Romance:

- Rekindling Romance: Rediscovering romance and intimacy in later life brings joy and revitalizes the relationship.

- Building New Memories: Creating new memories and shared experiences enhances the emotional bond and reinforces commitment.

Conclusion

Love and attraction in older adults are influenced by a complex interplay of biological, psychological, and social factors. Understanding these influences provides valuable insights into the dynamics of romantic relationships in later life.

Despite the challenges, older adults can experience deep emotional connections, mutual support, and personal growth in their romantic relationships. By embracing effective communication, prioritizing emotional and physical intimacy, and engaging in shared activities, older adults can maintain fulfilling and resilient partnerships.

As we continue to explore the dynamics of attraction and love across the lifespan, we gain a deeper appreciation for the enduring nature of human connection. This knowledge empowers individuals to cultivate meaningful and fulfilling relationships at any age, enhancing their overall well-being and happiness.

CHAPTER 08

THE SOCIAL SCIENCE OF ATTRACTION

Sociological Perspectives on Attraction

Attraction is not only influenced by biological and psychological factors but also deeply shaped by social and cultural contexts. Sociological perspectives on attraction examine how societal norms, cultural values, and social structures influence who we are attracted to and how we form romantic relationships. This chapter explores the social science of attraction, highlighting the role of socialization, cultural norms, social networks, and social stratification in shaping romantic preferences and behaviors.

Socialization and Attraction

Socialization is the process through which individuals learn and internalize the norms, values, and behaviors that are considered appropriate in their society. From a young age, socialization shapes our understanding of attraction and influences our romantic preferences.

Family Influence:

The family is one of the primary agents of socialization and plays a significant role in shaping romantic preferences and behaviors.

1. Parental Role Models:

   - Modeling Relationships: Children often model their understanding of relationships based on the dynamics they observe between their parents or caregivers. Healthy, supportive relationships can set positive examples, while conflictual or dysfunctional relationships can impact future romantic behaviors.

   - Parental Expectations: Parents may also communicate explicit expectations regarding appropriate partners, often based on cultural, religious, or social values. These expectations can influence individuals' choices in partners and their views on attraction.

2. Sibling Influence:

   - Observing Siblings: Older siblings can also serve as role models, influencing romantic behaviors and attitudes. Observing siblings' relationships provides additional insights into managing romantic dynamics.

Educational Systems:

Schools and educational institutions contribute to socialization by reinforcing societal norms and providing a social environment where early romantic relationships often begin.

1. Peer Relationships:

- Social Learning: Interaction with peers during school years helps shape romantic preferences and behaviors. Peer approval and acceptance can significantly influence whom individuals find attractive and how they approach relationships.

- Peer Pressure: Peer groups can exert pressure to conform to certain norms and behaviors, impacting romantic choices and actions.

2. Sex Education:

- Understanding Relationships: Comprehensive sex education programs that include information about healthy relationships, consent, and communication can positively influence romantic behaviors and attitudes.

- Challenging Stereotypes: Education can also challenge harmful stereotypes and promote more inclusive and respectful attitudes toward attraction and relationships.

Media and Popular Culture:

Media and popular culture are powerful agents of socialization, shaping perceptions of attractiveness and romantic norms through representations in television, movies, music, and social media.

1. Beauty Standards:

- Media Representations: Media often perpetuates specific beauty standards, influencing societal perceptions of physical attractiveness. These representations can impact self-esteem and shape preferences in romantic partners.

- Cultural Ideals: Popular culture also promotes certain cultural ideals and narratives about love and relationships, which can shape individuals' expectations and desires.

2. Romantic Narratives:

- Idealized Relationships: Romantic stories in movies, television shows, and literature often portray idealized versions of relationships, setting unrealistic expectations for real-life romance.

- Social Media Influences: Social media platforms can amplify these narratives, with curated portrayals of romance and attractiveness influencing users' perceptions and behaviors.

Cultural Norms and Attraction

Cultural norms and values play a crucial role in shaping romantic attraction and relationship behaviors. These norms can vary widely across different societies and influence who we find attractive and how we engage in romantic relationships.

Cultural Variability in Attraction:

Different cultures have distinct norms and values regarding what is considered attractive and desirable in a romantic partner.

1. Physical Attractiveness:

- Cultural Standards: Cultural standards of beauty and attractiveness can vary significantly. For example, while Western cultures often emphasize slimness and youthfulness, other cultures may value fuller body types or specific physical features.

- Traditional Dress and Adornments: Traditional dress and adornments can also influence perceptions of attractiveness. In many cultures, specific clothing, jewelry, or body modifications are considered attractive and signify cultural identity.

2. Behavioral Traits:

- Cultural Expectations: Different cultures prioritize different behavioral traits in romantic partners. For example, some cultures may value assertiveness and independence, while others may prioritize modesty and family-oriented behaviors.

- Gender Roles: Cultural norms around gender roles influence what traits are considered attractive. Traditional gender roles may emphasize masculinity and femininity, while more egalitarian cultures may value traits that support equality and partnership.

Cultural Practices and Rituals:

Cultural practices and rituals related to courtship and marriage shape how individuals experience attraction and form romantic relationships.

1. Courtship Rituals:

- Dating Practices: Cultural norms dictate acceptable behaviors and practices in dating. In some cultures, arranged marriages are common, while in others, dating and romantic relationships before marriage are the norm.

- Rituals and Traditions: Courtship rituals and traditions, such as formal introductions, family involvement, and ceremonial events, can influence the development of romantic relationships and the expression of attraction.

2. Marriage Norms:

- Marital Expectations: Cultural norms around marriage, including expectations for dowries, bride price, and familial approval, shape how romantic relationships progress to marriage.

- Social Obligations: Marriage may come with specific social obligations and roles, influencing how couples navigate their relationship and manage external pressures.

Social Networks and Attraction

Social networks, including family, friends, and community connections, play a significant role in romantic attraction and relationship formation. These networks provide opportunities for meeting potential partners and influence romantic choices.

Social Network Influence:

The influence of social networks on romantic relationships is multifaceted, impacting both the availability of potential partners and the social approval of relationships.

1. Introduction and Facilitation:

- Meeting Partners: Social networks often facilitate the meeting of potential partners through introductions, social gatherings, and community events. Friends and family play a key role in connecting individuals.

- Support and Approval: The approval and support of social networks can enhance relationship satisfaction and stability. Positive reinforcement from friends and family contributes to the perceived legitimacy and strength of the relationship.

2. Social Capital:

- Shared Connections: Shared social connections and mutual friends can strengthen romantic relationships by providing a support system and creating a sense of community.

- Resource Access: Social networks can provide access to resources, such as advice, emotional support, and practical assistance, enhancing relationship quality and resilience.

Social Network Constraints:

While social networks can facilitate romantic relationships, they can also impose constraints and limitations.

1. Social Norms and Expectations:

- Conformity Pressure: Social networks may exert pressure to conform to specific norms and expectations regarding romantic relationships, influencing partner choices and relationship behaviors.

- Stigma and Disapproval: Relationships that deviate from social norms, such as interracial or same-sex relationships, may face stigma and disapproval from social networks, creating additional challenges for the couple.

2. Geographic and Social Boundaries:

- Proximity and Accessibility: Social networks are often shaped by geographic and social boundaries, influencing the availability and accessibility of potential partners. Limited social networks can restrict romantic opportunities.

- Homophily: Social networks tend to be homophilous, meaning that individuals are more likely to associate with others who are similar to themselves in terms of social class, ethnicity, and interests. This homophily can influence romantic attraction and partner selection.

Social Stratification and Attraction

Social stratification, or the hierarchical arrangement of individuals in society based on factors such as socioeconomic status, education, and occupation, influences romantic attraction and partner selection. These stratification systems create distinct social groups with varying access to resources and opportunities, shaping romantic preferences and behaviors.

Socioeconomic Status:

Socioeconomic status (SES) plays a significant role in romantic attraction and relationship dynamics.

1. Partner Selection:

- Homogamy: Individuals often select partners with similar socioeconomic backgrounds, a phenomenon known as homogamy. Similar SES can provide shared experiences, values, and lifestyle expectations, enhancing relationship compatibility.

- Resource Considerations: Socioeconomic factors such as income, education, and occupation influence partner selection, as individuals may seek partners who can provide financial stability and social mobility.

2. Relationship Dynamics:

- Power and Control: Differences in socioeconomic status between partners can impact power dynamics and control within the relationship. Higher SES may confer greater decision-making power and influence.

- Financial Stress: Economic disparities and financial stress can create challenges in relationships, affecting communication, trust, and overall satisfaction.

Education and Occupation:

Educational attainment and occupational status also influence romantic attraction and relationship formation.

1. Educational Homogamy:

- Similar Backgrounds: Individuals often select partners with similar levels of education, reflecting shared intellectual interests and values. Educational homogamy can enhance communication and compatibility.

- Social Mobility: Higher levels of education are associated with greater social mobility and access to resources, influencing partner selection and relationship stability.

2. Work and Career:

- Work-Life Balance: The demands of work and career can impact romantic relationships, influencing the time and energy available for maintaining a partnership. Balancing work and personal life is crucial for relationship satisfaction.

- Occupational Similarity: Similar occupational fields and career goals can enhance relationship compatibility and mutual support. Partners in similar fields may better understand each other's professional challenges and aspirations.

Conclusion

Sociological perspectives on attraction provide a comprehensive understanding of how socialization, cultural norms, social networks, and social stratification influence romantic preferences and behaviors. These social factors shape who we find attractive, how we form relationships, and how we navigate the complexities of romantic dynamics.

By examining the social science of attraction, we gain valuable insights into the broader context of romantic relationships and the interplay between individual choices and societal influences. Understanding these

sociological dimensions empower individuals to navigate their romantic lives with greater awareness and intentionality, fostering healthier and more fulfilling connections.

As we continue to explore the multifaceted nature of attraction and love, we recognize the importance of considering the social and cultural contexts that shape our experiences. This knowledge enhances our ability to build meaningful and resilient relationships, ultimately enriching our overall well-being and happiness.

THE ROLE OF SOCIAL NORMS AND MEDIA IN SHAPING ATTRACTION

Attraction is a multifaceted phenomenon influenced by a blend of biological, psychological, and social factors. Among these, social norms and media play significant roles in shaping our perceptions of attractiveness and guiding our behaviors in romantic contexts. Social norms provide a framework of accepted behaviors and standards, while media reinforces and often creates these norms through various forms of representation. This chapter explores how social norms and media influence attraction, examining their impact on individual preferences, relationship dynamics, and societal trends.

Social Norms and Attraction

Social norms are the unwritten rules that govern behavior within a society. They influence how we perceive attractiveness, who we find attractive, and how we engage in romantic relationships.

Defining Social Norms:

Social norms can be explicit or implicit and encompass a wide range of behaviors and standards related to attraction and relationships.

1. Explicit Norms:

- Cultural Traditions: Explicit norms include cultural traditions and rituals related to courtship, dating, and marriage. These norms vary widely across cultures and influence how romantic relationships are initiated and maintained.

- Legal and Institutional Rules: Legal norms, such as age of consent and marriage laws, also shape romantic behaviors and societal expectations.

2. Implicit Norms:

- Social Expectations: Implicit norms are the unspoken social expectations about appropriate behavior in romantic contexts. These norms include expectations around gender roles, sexual behavior, and relationship progression.

- Peer Influence: Peer groups play a crucial role in reinforcing implicit norms by modeling behaviors and providing social feedback.

Impact of Social Norms on Attraction:

1. Gender Roles:

- Traditional Roles: Traditional gender roles prescribe specific behaviors and traits for men and women in romantic contexts. Men are often expected to be assertive and pursue partners, while women are encouraged to be nurturing and receptive.

- Evolving Roles: Evolving gender norms challenge traditional roles and promote more egalitarian relationships. These changes influence attraction by broadening the range of acceptable behaviors and traits for both genders.

2. Behavioral Expectations:

- Courtship Behaviors: Social norms dictate acceptable courtship behaviors, such as who should initiate contact, how dates should be conducted, and the appropriate level of physical intimacy. These expectations guide romantic interactions and influence attraction.

- Relationship Progression: Norms around the progression of relationships, including the timing of commitment, cohabitation, and marriage, shape how individuals navigate romantic partnerships.

3. Attractiveness Standards:

- Physical Appearance: Social norms establish standards of physical attractiveness, influencing preferences for body types, facial features, and grooming. These standards can vary by culture and change over time.

- Behavioral Traits: Norms also define attractive behavioral traits, such as confidence, kindness, and humor. These traits are often influenced by cultural values and societal expectations.

Media and Attraction

Media plays a powerful role in shaping social norms and influencing perceptions of attractiveness. Through various forms of representation, media reinforces existing norms and creates new ideals related to beauty, romance, and relationships.

Forms of Media Influence:

1. Television and Movies:

- Romantic Narratives: Television shows and movies often portray idealized versions of romantic relationships, setting unrealistic expectations for real-life romance. These narratives can shape viewers' perceptions of what constitutes a desirable partner and a successful relationship.

- Character Archetypes: Media representations frequently rely on character archetypes that reinforce specific gender roles and traits. These archetypes influence viewers' expectations and behaviors in romantic contexts.

2. Advertising and Marketing:

   - Beauty Standards: Advertising heavily influences standards of physical attractiveness by promoting specific body types, facial features, and grooming practices. These standards are often unattainable and can impact self-esteem and body image.

   - Consumer Behavior: Marketing strategies often leverage romantic and sexual imagery to sell products, reinforcing the association between certain traits or possessions and attractiveness.

3. Social Media:

   - Curated Representations: Social media platforms enable users to curate their representations, often presenting idealized versions of their lives and relationships. This curation can create pressure to conform to certain standards of attractiveness and relationship success.

   - Influencers and Trends: Social media influencers play a significant role in shaping trends related to beauty, fashion, and romance. Their influence can affect followers' perceptions and behaviors in romantic contexts.

Impact of Media on Attraction:

1. Idealized Beauty Standards:

   - Unrealistic Expectations: Media often promotes unrealistic beauty standards that can lead to dissatisfaction with one's appearance and the appearance of potential partners. These standards can impact self-esteem and romantic preferences.

- Cultural Homogenization: The global reach of media can lead to the homogenization of beauty standards, reducing cultural diversity in perceptions of attractiveness.

2. Relationship Expectations:

- Idealized Relationships: Media portrayals of romance often depict idealized relationships with minimal conflict and high levels of passion and fulfillment. These portrayals can create unrealistic expectations for real-life relationships.

- Pressure to Conform: Media representations can create pressure to conform to specific relationship milestones and behaviors, influencing how individuals navigate their romantic lives.

3. Social Comparison:

- Comparison and Self-Esteem: Media exposure can lead to social comparison, where individuals evaluate their appearance and relationships against idealized media representations. This comparison can negatively impact self-esteem and relationship satisfaction.

- Peer Influence: Social media, in particular, amplifies social comparison by providing a constant stream of curated content from peers. This influence can shape perceptions of attractiveness and romantic success.

Interplay Between Social Norms and Media

The relationship between social norms and media is reciprocal, with each influencing and reinforcing the other. Media both reflects and shapes societal norms, creating a dynamic interplay that continually evolves.

Media Reflecting Social Norms:

Media representations often reflect prevailing social norms and cultural values, reinforcing existing standards and behaviors.

1. Cultural Representation:

- Diverse Narratives: Media can reflect the diversity of cultural norms and values related to attraction and relationships, providing representation for different groups and experiences.

- Reinforcing Stereotypes: Conversely, media can also reinforce harmful stereotypes and perpetuate narrow standards of attractiveness and behavior.

2. Normative Influence:

- Reinforcement of Norms: By depicting certain behaviors and traits as desirable, media reinforces social norms and influences viewers' perceptions and actions.

- Normalization of Trends: Media can normalize emerging trends and behaviors, making them more widely accepted within society.

Media Shaping Social Norms:

Media has the power to shape social norms by introducing new ideas, challenging existing standards, and promoting alternative narratives.

1. Challenging Norms:

- Subversive Content: Media can challenge traditional norms and promote alternative representations of attraction and relationships, fostering greater acceptance of diversity and inclusivity.

- Cultural Shifts: Influential media content can drive cultural shifts by highlighting social issues, advocating for change, and inspiring new norms and behaviors.

2. Creating Trends:

- Fashion and Beauty Trends: Media often sets trends in fashion and beauty, influencing public perceptions of attractiveness and driving consumer behavior.

- Romantic Ideals: Romantic narratives and celebrity relationships can create new ideals and expectations for romantic relationships, shaping how individuals approach love and attraction.

Implications and Considerations

Understanding the role of social norms and media in shaping attraction has important implications for individuals and society. Recognizing these influences can help individuals navigate their romantic lives with greater awareness and critical thinking.

Individual Implications:

1. Self-Awareness:

- Critical Consumption: Developing media literacy and critically evaluating media content can help individuals recognize unrealistic portrayals and resist harmful social comparisons.

- Personal Standards: Reflecting on personal values and preferences can empower individuals to define their own standards of attractiveness and relationship goals, independent of societal pressures.

2. Mental Health:

- Body Image: Promoting positive body image and self-esteem involves challenging unrealistic beauty standards and embracing diverse representations of attractiveness.

- Relationship Satisfaction: Setting realistic expectations for relationships based on open communication and mutual respect can enhance relationship satisfaction and resilience.

Societal Implications:

1. Representation and Diversity:

- Inclusive Media: Promoting diverse and inclusive representations in media can challenge narrow standards of attractiveness and foster greater acceptance of different body types, identities, and relationship dynamics.

- Positive Role Models: Highlighting positive role models and healthy relationships in media can provide valuable examples for viewers and promote healthier romantic behaviors.

2. Cultural Change:

- Advocacy and Education: Advocating for media literacy education and raising awareness about the impact of social norms and media on attraction can empower individuals and drive cultural change.

- Policy and Regulation: Supporting policies and regulations that promote responsible media practices, such as accurate representation and ethical advertising, can mitigate the negative effects of media on attraction and relationships.

Conclusion

Social norms and media play pivotal roles in shaping our perceptions of attraction and guiding our romantic behaviors. By examining the influence of social norms and media, we gain a deeper understanding of the complex interplay between individual preferences and societal expectations.

Recognizing the impact of these social forces empowers individuals to navigate their romantic lives with greater awareness and intentionality, fostering healthier and more fulfilling connections. As we continue to explore the social science of attraction, we can work towards creating a more inclusive and supportive environment for diverse expressions of love and attractiveness.

This knowledge enhances our ability to build meaningful and resilient relationships, ultimately enriching our overall well-being and happiness.

ATTRACTION IN DIVERSE CULTURAL CONTEXTS

Attraction is a universal human experience, yet its expression and the traits considered attractive vary widely across different cultural contexts. These differences are shaped by cultural values, social norms, and historical influences that inform what people find appealing and desirable in romantic partners. This chapter explores how attraction manifests in diverse cultural contexts, examining the factors that influence romantic preferences and behaviors around the world.

Understanding Cultural Diversity in Attraction

Cultural diversity in attraction arises from the unique social, historical, and environmental contexts of different societies. These contexts shape the norms, values, and practices that influence how attraction is perceived and expressed.

Cultural Values and Norms:

Cultural values and norms play a crucial role in defining what is considered attractive and desirable in a romantic partner.

1. Individualism vs. Collectivism:

- Individualistic Cultures: In individualistic cultures, such as those in the United States and Western Europe, personal achievement, independence, and self-expression are highly valued. Traits like confidence, assertiveness, and individuality are often considered attractive.

- Collectivistic Cultures: In collectivistic cultures, such as those in East Asia and many parts of Africa, the well-being of the group, family, and community is prioritized. Traits like loyalty, humility, and social harmony are often valued and considered attractive.

2. Traditional vs. Modern Values:

- Traditional Societies: In societies with strong traditional values, attractiveness may be linked to adherence to cultural customs, familial duties, and religious practices. Gender roles may be more clearly defined, with distinct expectations for men and women.

- Modern Societies: In more modern or cosmopolitan societies, there may be greater emphasis on personal choice, equality, and self-fulfillment. These values can lead to more fluid and diverse standards of attractiveness.

Historical and Environmental Influences:

Historical events, geographic factors, and environmental conditions also shape cultural standards of attraction.

1. Historical Events:

- Colonial History: Colonial history has left lasting impacts on cultural perceptions of beauty and attraction, often introducing Western standards that can coexist or clash with traditional local norms.

- Migration and Diaspora: Migration and diaspora communities contribute to cultural exchange and hybridization, blending different standards of attractiveness and romantic practices.

2. Environmental Conditions:

- Climate and Resources: Environmental conditions, such as climate and availability of resources, influence cultural norms related to body types and physical traits. For instance, in regions where food scarcity has been a historical concern, a fuller body type might be seen as a sign of health and prosperity.

- Lifestyle and Occupations: The demands of daily life and common occupations can shape cultural preferences. For example, in agricultural societies, physical strength and endurance might be particularly valued.

Attraction in Various Cultural Contexts

Examining specific cultural contexts reveals the diversity in romantic preferences and the traits considered attractive around the world.

East Asian Cultures:

In East Asian cultures, such as those in China, Japan, and Korea, cultural values emphasize social harmony, respect for tradition, and collective well-being.

1. Physical Attractiveness:

- Fair Skin: Fair skin is often considered attractive, as it has historical associations with higher social status and indoor work, as opposed to manual labor outdoors.

- Youthful Appearance: A youthful appearance, including features like clear skin, big eyes, and a slender body, is highly valued.

2. Behavioral Traits:

- Modesty and Humility: Modesty and humility are highly regarded traits, reflecting the cultural emphasis on social harmony and respect for others.

- Educational and Career Success: In modern East Asian societies, educational and career achievements are also attractive traits, indicating diligence and the ability to provide a stable future.

South Asian Cultures:

In South Asian cultures, including those in India, Pakistan, and Bangladesh, cultural norms are deeply influenced by religious traditions, family structures, and social hierarchies.

1. Physical Attractiveness:

- Traditional Beauty Standards: Traditional beauty standards may include features such as long, dark hair, expressive eyes, and a fair complexion.

- Adherence to Traditional Dress: Wearing traditional attire, such as sarees for women and kurta-pajamas for men, can enhance attractiveness by signaling cultural and familial values.

2. Behavioral Traits:

- Family Orientation: Strong family ties and respect for elders are highly valued. Attractiveness is often linked to one's ability to integrate well into the extended family.

- Virtue and Modesty: Traits like virtue, modesty, and adherence to religious and cultural norms are considered important in a romantic partner.

Middle Eastern Cultures:

Middle Eastern cultures, including those in countries like Saudi Arabia, Iran, and Egypt, are influenced by Islamic traditions, historical empires, and contemporary social dynamics.

1. Physical Attractiveness:

- Emphasis on Eyes: In many Middle Eastern cultures, expressive eyes are a significant feature of attractiveness, often enhanced by traditional makeup techniques.

- Adornment and Dress: Adherence to cultural and religious dress codes, such as hijabs for women, can play a role in attractiveness by reflecting cultural identity and piety.

2. Behavioral Traits:

- Religious Devotion: Religious devotion and adherence to Islamic principles are highly valued traits, reflecting moral integrity and cultural commitment.

- Hospitality and Generosity: Traits like hospitality and generosity are important, reflecting the cultural emphasis on community and social responsibility.

African Cultures:

African cultures are diverse, encompassing a wide range of traditions and values across the continent. Common themes include the importance of community, traditional practices, and respect for elders.

1. Physical Attractiveness:

- Curvaceous Body Types: In many African cultures, fuller and curvaceous body types are considered attractive, symbolizing health, fertility, and prosperity.

- Hairstyles and Adornments: Traditional hairstyles and adornments, such as braids, beads, and scarification, are important aspects of cultural beauty.

2. Behavioral Traits:

- Community Orientation: Strong community ties and a sense of social responsibility are valued. Attractiveness is often linked to one's ability to contribute to and harmonize with the community.

- Respect for Tradition: Adherence to traditional customs and practices, including participation in cultural rituals and ceremonies, enhances attractiveness.

Western Cultures:

Western cultures, particularly in North America and Europe, emphasize individualism, personal achievement, and self-expression. These values shape contemporary standards of attraction.

1. Physical Attractiveness:

- Slim and Fit Body Types: Slim and fit body types are often emphasized, reflecting cultural ideals related to health, fitness, and self-discipline.

- Youthful Appearance: Youthfulness is highly valued, with significant emphasis on skincare, fashion, and anti-aging products.

2. Behavioral Traits:

- Confidence and Independence: Confidence, independence, and assertiveness are attractive traits, reflecting the cultural emphasis on self-reliance and personal success.

- Openness and Expressiveness: Traits like openness, expressiveness, and a sense of humor are valued, promoting emotional connection and social engagement.

Globalization and Cultural Hybridization

Globalization has facilitated cultural exchange and interaction, leading to the hybridization of cultural norms and standards of attraction. This process creates a dynamic interplay between traditional values and modern influences.

Cultural Exchange:

1. Media and Popular Culture:

- Global Media Influence: Global media, including movies, television, and social media, disseminates cultural standards of beauty and romance across borders, blending different cultural ideals.

- Celebrity Influence: International celebrities and influencers play a significant role in shaping global trends, often promoting a mix of cultural aesthetics.

2. Migration and Diaspora Communities:

- Cultural Blending: Migration and the presence of diaspora communities contribute to the blending of cultural norms and practices, creating diverse standards of attractiveness within multicultural societies.

- Intercultural Relationships: Intercultural relationships provide opportunities for cultural exchange and the integration of different romantic traditions and values.

Cultural Hybridization:

1. Adapting and Integrating Norms:

- Syncretism: Cultural hybridization often involves syncretism, where traditional and modern elements merge to create new standards and practices. This process can lead to more inclusive and diverse perceptions of attraction.

- Evolving Standards: As cultures interact and adapt, standards of attraction evolve, reflecting changing values and societal dynamics.

2. Challenging Stereotypes:

- Promoting Diversity: Cultural hybridization challenges narrow and monolithic standards of beauty and attraction, promoting a broader appreciation of diversity and individuality.

- Redefining Attractiveness: By embracing multiple cultural influences, societies can redefine attractiveness in ways that are more inclusive and representative of global diversity.

Conclusion

Attraction in diverse cultural contexts is shaped by a complex interplay of cultural values, social norms, historical influences, and environmental conditions. Understanding these diverse perspectives provides valuable insights into the richness and variability of human attraction.

As globalization continues to facilitate cultural exchange, the hybridization of cultural norms and standards of attractiveness presents both challenges and opportunities. Embracing cultural diversity and promoting inclusive standards of beauty and romance can enhance mutual understanding and appreciation across different societies.

By exploring the social science of attraction in diverse cultural contexts, we gain a deeper appreciation for the multifaceted nature of human relationships and the factors that shape our romantic preferences and behaviors. This knowledge empowers individuals to navigate their romantic lives with greater awareness and respect for cultural diversity, fostering healthier and more fulfilling connections.

As we continue to examine the dynamics of attraction and love across different cultural landscapes, we recognize the importance of cultural sensitivity

and inclusivity in building meaningful and resilient relationships. This understanding ultimately enriches our overall well-being and happiness, enhancing our ability to connect with others in profound and meaningful ways.

ATTRACTION IN DIVERSE CULTURAL CONTEXTS

Attraction is a universal human experience, but its expression and the traits considered attractive vary widely across different cultural contexts. These differences are shaped by cultural values, social norms, and historical influences that inform what people find appealing and desirable in romantic partners. This chapter explores how attraction manifests in diverse cultural contexts, examining the factors that influence romantic preferences and behaviors around the world

Cultural Values and Norms

Cultural values and norms play a crucial role in defining what is considered attractive and desirable in a romantic partner.

Individualism vs. Collectivism:

- Individualistic Cultures: In individualistic cultures, such as those in the United States and Western Europe, personal achievement, independence, and self-expression are highly valued. Traits like confidence, assertiveness, and individuality are often considered attractive.

- Collectivistic Cultures: In collectivistic cultures, such as those in East Asia and many parts of Africa, the well-being of the group, family, and community is prioritized. Traits like loyalty, humility, and social harmony are often valued and considered attractive.

Traditional vs. Modern Values:

- Traditional Societies: In societies with strong traditional values, attractiveness may be linked to adherence to cultural customs, familial duties, and religious practices. Gender roles may be more clearly defined, with distinct expectations for men and women.

- Modern Societies: In more modern or cosmopolitan societies, there may be greater emphasis on personal choice, equality, and self-fulfillment. These values can lead to more fluid and diverse standards of attractiveness.

Historical and Environmental Influences

Historical events, geographic factors, and environmental conditions also shape cultural standards of attraction.

Historical Events:

- Colonial History: Colonial history has left lasting impacts on cultural perceptions of beauty and attraction, often introducing Western standards that can coexist or clash with traditional local norms.

- Migration and Diaspora: Migration and diaspora communities contribute to cultural exchange and hybridization, blending different standards of attractiveness and romantic practices.

Environmental Conditions:

- Climate and Resources: Environmental conditions, such as climate and availability of resources, influence cultural norms related to body types and physical traits. For instance, in regions where food scarcity has been a historical concern, a fuller body type might be seen as a sign of health and prosperity.

- Lifestyle and Occupations: The demands of daily life and common occupations can shape cultural preferences. For example, in agricultural societies, physical strength and endurance might be particularly valued.

Attraction in Various Cultural Contexts

Examining specific cultural contexts reveals the diversity in romantic preferences and the traits considered attractive around the world.

East Asian Cultures:

In East Asian cultures, such as those in China, Japan, and Korea, cultural values emphasize social harmony, respect for tradition, and collective well-being.

- Physical Attractiveness: Fair skin, a youthful appearance, and a slender body are often considered attractive. These traits are associated with higher social status and health.

- Behavioral Traits: Modesty, humility, and educational and career success are highly valued. These traits reflect the cultural emphasis on social harmony, respect for others, and diligence.

South Asian Cultures:

In South Asian cultures, including those in India, Pakistan, and Bangladesh, cultural norms are deeply influenced by religious traditions, family structures, and social hierarchies.

- Physical Attractiveness: Traditional beauty standards may include features such as long, dark hair, expressive eyes, and a fair complexion. Wearing traditional attire can enhance attractiveness by signaling cultural and familial values.

- Behavioral Traits: Strong family ties, respect for elders, virtue, and modesty are highly valued. These traits reflect the cultural emphasis on family orientation and adherence to religious and cultural norms.

Middle Eastern Cultures:

Middle Eastern cultures, including those in countries like Saudi Arabia, Iran, and Egypt, are influenced by Islamic traditions, historical empires, and contemporary social dynamics.

- Physical Attractiveness: Expressive eyes, often enhanced by traditional makeup techniques, are a significant feature of attractiveness. Adherence to cultural and religious dress codes can also play a role in attractiveness by reflecting cultural identity and piety.

- Behavioral Traits: Religious devotion, hospitality, and generosity are highly valued. These traits reflect the cultural emphasis on moral integrity, community, and social responsibility.

African Cultures:

African cultures are diverse, encompassing a wide range of traditions and values across the continent. Common themes include the importance of community, traditional practices, and respect for elders.

- Physical Attractiveness: Fuller and curvaceous body types are often considered attractive, symbolizing health, fertility, and prosperity. Traditional hairstyles and adornments, such as braids, beads, and scarification, are important aspects of cultural beauty.

- Behavioral Traits: Strong community ties, social responsibility, and adherence to traditional customs and practices are highly valued. These traits reflect the cultural emphasis on community orientation and respect for tradition.

Western Cultures:

Western cultures, particularly in North America and Europe, emphasize individualism, personal achievement, and self-expression. These values shape contemporary standards of attraction.

- Physical Attractiveness: Slim and fit body types, youthfulness, and fashion-forward appearance are often emphasized. These traits reflect cultural ideals related to health, fitness, and self-discipline.

- Behavioral Traits: Confidence, independence, and assertiveness are attractive traits, reflecting the cultural emphasis on self-reliance and personal success. Openness, expressiveness, and a sense of humor are also highly valued.

Globalization and Cultural Hybridization

Globalization has facilitated cultural exchange and interaction, leading to the hybridization of cultural norms and standards of attraction. This process creates a dynamic interplay between traditional values and modern influences.

Cultural Exchange:

- Media and Popular Culture: Global media, including movies, television, and social media, disseminates cultural standards of beauty and romance across borders, blending different cultural ideals. International celebrities and influencers play a significant role in shaping global trends.

- Migration and Diaspora Communities: Migration and the presence of diaspora communities contribute to the blending of cultural norms and practices, creating diverse standards of attractiveness within multicultural societies. Intercultural relationships provide opportunities for cultural exchange and the integration of different romantic traditions and values.

Cultural Hybridization:

- Adapting and Integrating Norms: Cultural hybridization often involves syncretism, where traditional and modern elements merge to create new standards and practices. This process can lead to more inclusive and diverse perceptions of attraction.

- Challenging Stereotypes: Cultural hybridization challenges narrow and monolithic standards of beauty and attraction, promoting a broader appreciation of diversity and individuality. By embracing multiple cultural influences, societies can redefine attractiveness in ways that are more inclusive and representative of global diversity.

Conclusion

Attraction in diverse cultural contexts is shaped by a complex interplay of cultural values, social norms, historical influences, and environmental conditions. Understanding these diverse perspectives provides valuable insights into the richness and variability of human attraction.

As globalization continues to facilitate cultural exchange, the hybridization of cultural norms and standards of attractiveness presents both challenges and opportunities. Embracing cultural diversity and promoting inclusive standards of beauty and romance can enhance mutual understanding and appreciation across different societies.

By exploring the social science of attraction in diverse cultural contexts, we gain a deeper appreciation for the multifaceted nature of human relationships and the factors that shape our romantic preferences and behaviors. This knowledge empowers individuals to navigate their romantic lives with greater awareness and respect for cultural diversity, fostering healthier and more fulfilling connections.

As we continue to examine the dynamics of attraction and love across different cultural landscapes, we recognize the importance of cultural sensitivity and inclusivity in building meaningful and resilient relationships. This understanding ultimately enriches our overall well-being and happiness, enhancing our ability to connect with others in profound and meaningful ways.

CHAPTER 09

CHALLENGES TO ATTRACTION

Psychological Disorders and Their Impact on Attraction

Attraction and romantic relationships are complex processes influenced by a multitude of factors, including psychological well-being. Psychological disorders can significantly impact an individual's experience of attraction and their ability to form and maintain romantic relationships. This chapter explores the ways in which various psychological disorders affect attraction, highlighting the challenges individuals face and offering insights into managing these difficulties to foster healthier relationships.

Understanding Psychological Disorders

Psychological disorders, also known as mental health disorders, are conditions that affect an individual's mood, thinking, behavior, and overall mental functioning. These disorders can range from anxiety and depression to more severe conditions like bipolar disorder and schizophrenia.

Common Psychological Disorders Affecting Attraction:

1. Anxiety Disorders:

- Generalized Anxiety Disorder (GAD): Characterized by excessive and persistent worry about various aspects of life.

- Social Anxiety Disorder: Intense fear of social situations, leading to avoidance and distress.

- Panic Disorder: Recurrent panic attacks and the fear of having more attacks.

2. Mood Disorders:

- Depression: Persistent feelings of sadness, hopelessness, and a lack of interest or pleasure in activities.

- Bipolar Disorder: Alternating periods of depression and mania, characterized by extreme mood swings.

3. Personality Disorders:

- Borderline Personality Disorder (BPD): Instability in relationships, self-image, and emotions, along with impulsive behaviors.

- Narcissistic Personality Disorder (NPD): Grandiosity, a need for admiration, and a lack of empathy for others.

4. Obsessive-Compulsive Disorder (OCD):

- Obsessions and Compulsions: Recurrent, intrusive thoughts (obsessions) and repetitive behaviors (compulsions) aimed at reducing anxiety.

5. Schizophrenia and Psychotic Disorders:

- Delusions and Hallucinations: Distorted thinking, false beliefs, and sensory experiences that are not based in reality.

Impact of Psychological Disorders on Attraction

Psychological disorders can affect attraction and romantic relationships in various ways, influencing an individual's ability to connect with others, manage emotions, and maintain stable relationships.

Anxiety Disorders:

1. Generalized Anxiety Disorder (GAD):

- Impact on Attraction: Constant worry and fear can make it difficult to relax and enjoy social interactions, reducing opportunities for forming romantic connections.

- Relationship Challenges: Individuals with GAD may seek excessive reassurance from partners, leading to strain in the relationship.

2. Social Anxiety Disorder:

- Impact on Attraction: Intense fear of social situations can hinder the ability to meet new people and develop romantic interests.

- Avoidance Behavior: Avoidance of social interactions can limit opportunities for dating and forming meaningful connections.

3. Panic Disorder:

- Impact on Attraction: The fear of experiencing panic attacks in social settings can lead to avoidance of romantic situations.

- Relationship Strain: Partners may struggle to understand and support the individual's need to avoid certain environments.

Mood Disorders:

1. Depression:

- Impact on Attraction: Persistent sadness and lack of interest in activities can diminish the desire to seek out romantic relationships.

- Low Self-Esteem: Negative self-perception and feelings of worthlessness can hinder confidence in pursuing romantic interests.

2. Bipolar Disorder:

- Impact on Attraction: Mood swings can lead to inconsistent behavior, making it challenging to form and maintain stable relationships.

- Relationship Instability: Periods of mania may involve risky behaviors, while depressive episodes can lead to withdrawal and emotional unavailability.

Personality Disorders:

1. Borderline Personality Disorder (BPD):

- Impact on Attraction: Intense emotions and fear of abandonment can lead to turbulent and unstable relationships.

- Relationship Dynamics: Individuals with BPD may experience rapid shifts between idealizing and devaluing their partners, creating a roller-coaster dynamic.

2. Narcissistic Personality Disorder (NPD):

- Impact on Attraction: Grandiosity and a lack of empathy can make forming genuine emotional connections difficult.

- Relationship Issues: Partners may feel undervalued and neglected due to the individual's constant need for admiration and validation.

Obsessive-Compulsive Disorder (OCD):

- Impact on Attraction: Obsessions and compulsions can dominate an individual's life, leaving little room for social interactions and romantic pursuits.

- Relationship Challenges: Partners may struggle to understand the nature of the obsessions and compulsions, leading to frustration and miscommunication.

Schizophrenia and Psychotic Disorders:

- Impact on Attraction: Delusions and hallucinations can distort an individual's perception of reality, making it challenging to form and maintain relationships.

- Social Isolation: The symptoms of psychotic disorders can lead to social withdrawal and isolation, reducing opportunities for romantic connections.

Strategies for Managing the Impact of Psychological Disorders on Attraction

While psychological disorders present significant challenges, individuals can take steps to manage their symptoms and improve their romantic relationships. Support from mental health professionals, effective communication, and self-care practices are crucial for fostering healthier connections.

Seeking Professional Help:

1. Therapy and Counseling:

- Cognitive-Behavioral Therapy (CBT): CBT can help individuals with anxiety and mood disorders identify and change negative thought patterns, improving their ability to engage in social interactions and romantic relationships.

- Dialectical Behavior Therapy (DBT): DBT is particularly effective for individuals with BPD, helping them develop skills for managing emotions and improving relationship dynamics.

2. Medication:

- Psychotropic Medications: Medications such as antidepressants, mood stabilizers, and antipsychotics can help manage symptoms of psychological disorders, making it easier to participate in romantic relationships.

Improving Communication:

1. Open and Honest Dialogue:

- Discussing Mental Health: Openly discussing mental health with romantic partners can foster understanding and support. Partners who are aware of the challenges can better empathize and provide assistance.

- Setting Boundaries: Establishing clear boundaries and communicating needs can prevent misunderstandings and reduce relationship strain.

2. Active Listening:

- Empathy and Validation: Practicing active listening and showing empathy can strengthen the emotional connection between partners. Validation of each other's feelings is crucial for maintaining a supportive relationship.

Building Self-Esteem and Confidence:

1. Self-Care Practices:

- Physical Health: Regular exercise, a balanced diet, and adequate sleep are essential for overall well-being and can improve mood and energy levels.

- Mindfulness and Relaxation: Mindfulness practices, such as meditation and deep breathing, can help manage anxiety and stress, enhancing emotional stability.

2. Personal Growth:

- Setting Achievable Goals: Setting and achieving personal goals can boost self-esteem and confidence, making it easier to pursue romantic interests.

- Engaging in Hobbies: Participating in activities that bring joy and fulfillment can improve mood and provide opportunities to meet potential partners.

Building and Maintaining Relationships:

1. Developing Trust:

- Consistency and Reliability: Building trust involves being consistent and reliable in actions and communication. Trust is the foundation of a healthy relationship.

- Transparency: Being transparent about mental health struggles and progress helps partners understand and support each other better.

2. Managing Conflict:

- Conflict Resolution Skills: Learning and practicing conflict resolution skills can prevent misunderstandings from escalating and damaging the relationship.

- Seeking Support: Couples therapy can provide a safe space to address relationship challenges and develop effective strategies for managing conflicts.

Support Systems and Resources

Building a strong support system is crucial for individuals with psychological disorders to navigate the challenges of attraction and relationships. Friends, family, and mental health professionals can provide essential support and guidance.

Friends and Family:

1. Emotional Support:

- Understanding and Empathy: Friends and family who understand the individual's struggles can offer emotional support and encouragement, helping them feel less isolated.

- Practical Assistance: Providing practical assistance, such as helping with daily tasks or accompanying the individual to social events, can reduce anxiety and increase opportunities for social interactions.

2. Encouragement and Motivation:

- Positive Reinforcement: Encouraging and reinforcing positive behaviors and achievements can boost self-esteem and confidence.

- Involvement in Activities: Inviting individuals to participate in social activities and gatherings can help them build social skills and expand their social network.

Mental Health Professionals:

1. Therapists and Counselors:

- Individual Therapy: One-on-one therapy sessions can provide a safe space for individuals to explore their feelings, develop coping strategies, and work towards personal growth.

- Group Therapy: Group therapy offers opportunities to connect with others facing similar challenges, providing support and reducing feelings of isolation.

2. Psychiatrists:

- Medication Management: Psychiatrists can prescribe and manage medications that help control symptoms, improving overall functioning and relationship quality.

- Regular Check-Ins: Regular appointments with a psychiatrist ensure that treatment plans are effective and adjusted as needed.

Support Groups and Community Resources:

1. Support Groups:

- Peer Support: Support groups provide a platform for individuals to share their experiences, gain insights, and receive encouragement from peers who understand their struggles.

- Resource Sharing: These groups often share resources, such as coping strategies and information about mental health services, which can be beneficial for managing symptoms and improving relationships.

2. Community Programs:

- Workshops and Seminars: Community programs that offer workshops and seminars on mental health, relationship skills, and self-care can provide valuable knowledge and support.

- Social Events: Participating in community social events can help individuals build connections and practice social skills in a supportive environment.

Conclusion

Psychological disorders present significant challenges to attraction and romantic relationships, affecting individuals' ability to connect with others, manage emotions, and maintain stable partnerships. However, with the right support, strategies, and resources, individuals with psychological disorders can navigate these challenges and foster healthy, fulfilling relationships.

Understanding the impact of psychological disorders on attraction is crucial for developing empathy and providing appropriate support to those affected. By seeking professional help, improving communication, building self-esteem, and leveraging support systems, individuals can overcome the barriers posed by psychological disorders and experience meaningful romantic connections.

As we continue to explore the dynamics of attraction and relationships, it is essential to recognize the diverse experiences of individuals with psychological disorders and promote a compassionate, inclusive approach to mental health and romantic relationships. This understanding ultimately enriches our ability to connect with others in profound and meaningful ways, enhancing our overall well-being and happiness.

EXTERNAL FACTORS: STRESS AND SOCIOECONOMIC STATUS

Attraction and romantic relationships are not only influenced by personal attributes and psychological factors but also significantly shaped by external factors such as stress and socioeconomic status. These factors can affect individuals' ability to form and maintain romantic connections, impacting relationship satisfaction and stability. This chapter explores how stress and socioeconomic status influence attraction and relationships, highlighting the challenges they pose and offering strategies for managing their impact.

The Impact of Stress on Attraction and Relationships

Stress is a common aspect of modern life, arising from various sources such as work, finances, health, and interpersonal relationships. Chronic stress can have profound effects on physical and mental health, which in turn can influence attraction and relationship dynamics.

Sources of Stress:

1. Work-Related Stress:

- Job Demands: High job demands, long working hours, and job insecurity can contribute to significant stress, leaving individuals with less time and energy for romantic relationships.

- Work-Life Balance: Struggling to balance work responsibilities with personal life can strain relationships and reduce opportunities for intimacy and connection.

2. Financial Stress:

- Economic Insecurity: Concerns about financial stability, debt, and expenses can create ongoing stress, impacting individuals' ability to focus on and invest in their relationships.

- Disparities in Income: Disparities in income between partners can lead to power imbalances and conflicts, affecting relationship satisfaction.

3. Health-Related Stress:

- Chronic Illness: Managing chronic health conditions can be stressful, affecting individuals' mood, energy levels, and ability to engage in romantic activities.

- Caregiving Responsibilities: Caring for a sick or elderly family member can add significant stress and reduce the time available for nurturing romantic relationships.

4. Interpersonal Stress:

- Family Conflicts: Conflicts with family members, including in-laws, can create additional stress and tension in romantic relationships.

- Social Pressure: Societal expectations and peer pressure regarding relationship milestones (e.g., marriage, having children) can contribute to stress and anxiety.

Effects of Stress on Attraction and Relationships:

1. Emotional and Physical Well-Being:

- Emotional Strain: Chronic stress can lead to emotional exhaustion, anxiety, and depression, which can diminish individuals' capacity to engage in and enjoy romantic relationships.

- Physical Health: Stress can negatively impact physical health, leading to issues such as fatigue, insomnia, and weakened immune function, which can reduce individuals' attractiveness and availability for romantic activities.

2. Relationship Dynamics:

- Communication Breakdowns: Stress can impair communication, leading to misunderstandings, increased conflicts, and decreased emotional intimacy between partners.

- Reduced Intimacy: High stress levels can reduce libido and physical intimacy, impacting the overall quality of the relationship.

3. Attraction and Preferences:

- Perceived Attractiveness: Stress can affect self-esteem and body image, influencing how individuals perceive their own attractiveness and their attractiveness to others.

- Partner Preferences: Stress may shift partner preferences, with individuals seeking stability and support to mitigate their stress.

Strategies for Managing Stress in Relationships:

1. Stress Management Techniques:

- Mindfulness and Relaxation: Practices such as mindfulness meditation, deep breathing exercises, and yoga can help reduce stress and improve emotional regulation.

- Regular Exercise: Physical activity is an effective way to manage stress, boost mood, and enhance overall well-being.

2. Effective Communication:

- Open Dialogue: Discussing stressors with a partner can foster understanding and support, reducing the emotional burden of stress.

- Active Listening: Practicing active listening and empathy can help partners feel heard and validated, strengthening the emotional connection.

3. Work-Life Balance:

- Setting Boundaries: Establishing boundaries between work and personal life can help reduce work-related stress and create more time for relationship activities.

- Prioritizing Quality Time: Scheduling regular quality time with a partner can strengthen the relationship and provide a buffer against stress.

4. Financial Planning:

- Budgeting and Planning: Developing a budget and financial plan can alleviate financial stress and promote a sense of security and stability in the relationship.

- Seeking Financial Advice: Consulting with a financial advisor can provide strategies for managing debt and improving financial health.

The Impact of Socioeconomic Status on Attraction and Relationships

Socioeconomic status (SES) encompasses individuals' economic and social position, influenced by factors such as income, education, and occupation. SES significantly affects various aspects of life, including health, opportunities, and social interactions, which in turn influence attraction and romantic relationships.

Components of Socioeconomic Status:

1. Income:

- Economic Resources: Income determines the level of economic resources available for lifestyle choices, leisure activities, and relationship investments.

- Financial Stability: Higher income levels are often associated with greater financial stability and security, which can enhance relationship satisfaction.

2. Education:

- Educational Attainment: Education influences knowledge, skills, and perspectives, shaping individuals' values, interests, and partner preferences.

- Social Mobility: Higher educational attainment is often linked to better job prospects and social mobility, impacting relationship dynamics and opportunities.

3. Occupation:

- Job Prestige: Occupational status can affect social standing, self-esteem, and perceived attractiveness.

- Work Environment: The nature of one's job, including working conditions and job stress, can influence relationship quality and satisfaction.

Effects of Socioeconomic Status on Attraction and Relationships:

1. Partner Selection:

- Homogamy: Individuals often select partners with similar SES, a phenomenon known as homogamy. Similar educational and economic backgrounds can enhance compatibility and mutual understanding.

- Resource Considerations: SES influences partner preferences, with individuals often seeking partners who can provide financial stability and social mobility.

2. Relationship Dynamics:

- Power Imbalances: Disparities in SES between partners can create power imbalances and conflicts, affecting relationship satisfaction and stability.

- Financial Stress: Financial difficulties and economic insecurity can strain relationships, leading to increased conflicts and reduced relationship quality.

3. Social and Cultural Capital:

- Shared Interests and Values: Similar SES often correlates with shared cultural capital, including interests, hobbies, and values, which can enhance relationship compatibility.

- Social Networks: SES influences social networks and opportunities for social interactions, affecting the availability and selection of potential partners.

Strategies for Addressing Socioeconomic Challenges in Relationships:

1. Open Communication:

- Discussing SES Differences: Openly discussing SES differences and their impact on the relationship can foster understanding and mitigate potential conflicts.

- Setting Financial Goals: Collaboratively setting financial goals and planning for the future can enhance financial stability and relationship satisfaction.

2. Building Financial Literacy:

- Financial Education: Increasing financial literacy through education and resources can help individuals manage their finances more effectively and reduce financial stress.

- Budgeting and Saving: Developing a budget and saving plan can promote financial security and reduce the impact of economic disparities on the relationship.

3. Seeking Support:

- Counseling and Therapy: Relationship counseling can provide tools and strategies for managing SES-related conflicts and improving relationship dynamics.

- Community Resources: Accessing community resources, such as financial assistance programs and social services, can alleviate economic pressures and support relationship well-being.

4. Promoting Social Mobility:

- Educational Opportunities: Pursuing educational opportunities and career advancement can improve SES and enhance relationship prospects.

- Networking and Mentorship: Building social networks and seeking mentorship can provide support and opportunities for social and economic mobility.

Conclusion

External factors such as stress and socioeconomic status play significant roles in shaping attraction and romantic relationships. Understanding the impact of these factors is crucial for addressing the challenges they pose and fostering healthier, more fulfilling connections.

By managing stress through effective communication, stress reduction techniques, and work-life balance, individuals can improve their emotional and physical well-being, enhancing their ability to engage in and maintain romantic relationships. Addressing socioeconomic challenges through open communication, financial literacy, and support systems can mitigate conflicts and promote relationship satisfaction.

As we continue to explore the dynamics of attraction and relationships, it is essential to recognize the influence of external factors and develop strategies to navigate them effectively. This understanding empowers individuals to build resilient and meaningful connections, ultimately enriching their overall well-being and happiness.

INFIDELITY AND ITS EFFECTS ON ATTRACTION AND RELATIONSHIP

Infidelity, or unfaithfulness in a committed relationship, is one of the most challenging and distressing issues couples can face. It can have profound effects on attraction, trust, and the overall dynamics of a relationship. This chapter explores the various dimensions of infidelity, its impact on attraction and relationships, and strategies for coping and recovery.

Understanding Infidelity

Infidelity can take various forms, ranging from emotional affairs to physical intimacy with someone outside the committed relationship. Understanding the different types and motivations behind infidelity can help in addressing its impact.

Types of Infidelity:

1. Emotional Infidelity:

- Emotional Bonding: Involves forming a deep emotional connection with someone other than the partner. This can include sharing personal thoughts, feelings, and intimate details.

- Emotional Affairs: Often start as friendships that gradually develop into something deeper, potentially leading to secrecy and feelings of betrayal.

2. Physical Infidelity:

- Sexual Encounters: Involves engaging in sexual activities with someone other than the committed partner. This can range from one-night stands to ongoing sexual relationships.

- Online Infidelity: Includes engaging in sexual conversations, exchanging explicit content, or maintaining virtual relationships through digital platforms.

3. Combined Infidelity:

- Emotional and Physical Affairs: Some instances of infidelity involve both emotional and physical connections, which can be particularly damaging due to the deep bond formed outside the primary relationship.

Motivations Behind Infidelity:

1. Emotional Needs:

- Lack of Emotional Fulfillment: Individuals may seek emotional intimacy and validation outside the relationship if they feel emotionally neglected or unappreciated by their partner.

- Desire for Novelty: The excitement and novelty of a new emotional connection can be enticing, especially if the primary relationship feels stagnant.

2. Physical Desires:

- Sexual Dissatisfaction: Unmet sexual needs or dissatisfaction with the physical aspect of the relationship can lead individuals to seek sexual fulfillment elsewhere.

- Curiosity and Variety: A desire for sexual variety or curiosity about other partners can drive individuals to engage in physical infidelity.

3. Personal Factors:

- Self-Esteem Issues: Individuals with low self-esteem may seek external validation through infidelity to boost their self-worth.

- Opportunity and Temptation: Situational factors, such as being away from the partner for extended periods or encountering tempting opportunities, can lead to infidelity.

4. Relationship Dynamics:

- Conflict and Resentment: Ongoing conflicts, unresolved issues, and feelings of resentment within the relationship can push individuals toward infidelity as a form of escape or retaliation.

- Lack of Commitment: A weaker commitment to the relationship or doubts about its future can make infidelity seem less consequential.

Effects of Infidelity on Attraction and Relationships

Infidelity can have devastating effects on the individuals involved and the overall dynamics of the relationship. The impact varies depending on the nature of the infidelity, the existing relationship dynamics, and the responses of both partners.

Impact on Trust and Emotional Intimacy:

1. Loss of Trust:

- Betrayal: Infidelity is often perceived as a profound betrayal, leading to a significant loss of trust. Trust is a cornerstone of any relationship, and its erosion can create a sense of instability and insecurity.

- Doubt and Suspicion: Even after infidelity is revealed, doubts and suspicions about the partner's actions and intentions can persist, further straining the relationship.

2. Emotional Pain:

- Feelings of Hurt and Anger: The partner who has been betrayed often experiences intense emotional pain, including feelings of hurt, anger, and sadness. These emotions can overwhelm the relationship and make communication difficult.

- Self-Esteem Issues: Infidelity can also lead to feelings of inadequacy and lowered self-esteem in the betrayed partner, who may question their own worth and attractiveness.

3. Emotional Distance:

- Withdrawal: In response to the pain and betrayal, the betrayed partner may emotionally withdraw from the relationship, creating a distance that is difficult to bridge.

- Fear of Vulnerability: Fear of being hurt again can make both partners hesitant to be emotionally vulnerable, hindering the rebuilding of intimacy and connection.

Impact on Relationship Dynamics:

1. Communication Breakdown:

- Avoidance of Discussion: Infidelity often leads to a breakdown in communication, with both partners avoiding difficult discussions about the betrayal and its impact.

- Increased Conflict: When communication does occur, it may be marked by increased conflict, blame, and defensiveness, making it challenging to resolve issues constructively.

2. Changes in Attraction:

- Diminished Attraction: The emotional fallout from infidelity can lead to a decrease in physical and emotional attraction between partners, as feelings of love and desire are overshadowed by pain and betrayal.

- Altered Perceptions: The betrayed partner may struggle to see the unfaithful partner in the same light, affecting their overall perception of attractiveness and desirability.

. Relationship Instability:

- Uncertainty about the Future: Infidelity can create uncertainty about the future of the relationship, with both partners questioning whether they can rebuild trust and move forward together.

- Increased Likelihood of Separation: The strain of dealing with infidelity can increase the likelihood of separation or divorce, especially if both partners are unable or unwilling to work through the issues.

Impact on Individual Well-Being:

1. Mental Health Issues:

- Anxiety and Depression: The emotional turmoil caused by infidelity can lead to mental health issues such as anxiety and depression, affecting both partners' overall well-being.

- Stress and Trauma: Infidelity can be a traumatic experience, leading to heightened stress levels and symptoms of post-traumatic stress disorder (PTSD) in some individuals.

2. Behavioral Changes:

- Changes in Behavior: Both partners may exhibit changes in behavior, such as increased irritability, withdrawal from social activities, or changes in sleeping and eating patterns.

- Coping Mechanisms: Some individuals may turn to unhealthy coping mechanisms, such as substance abuse or avoidance, to deal with the pain and stress of infidelity.

Coping with Infidelity and Moving Forward

While infidelity can have devastating effects on a relationship, it is possible for couples to cope with the aftermath and work towards rebuilding trust and intimacy. The process requires commitment, effort, and often the support of professionals.

Strategies for Coping with Infidelity:

1. Open Communication:

- Honest Discussions: Open and honest discussions about the infidelity, its impact, and the underlying issues are crucial for healing. Both partners need to express their feelings and listen to each other with empathy.

- Avoiding Blame: While it is important to address the hurt and betrayal, focusing on blame can hinder the healing process. Constructive communication involves addressing the issues without assigning excessive blame.

2. Seeking Professional Help:

- Couples Therapy: Professional counseling can provide a safe space for couples to explore their feelings, understand the reasons behind the infidelity, and develop strategies for rebuilding trust.

- Individual Therapy: Individual therapy can help both partners work through their emotions, build self-esteem, and develop healthier coping mechanisms.

3. Rebuilding Trust:

- Consistency and Reliability: Rebuilding trust requires consistent and reliable behavior from the unfaithful partner. Demonstrating commitment and transparency can help restore the sense of security in the relationship.

- Setting Boundaries: Establishing clear boundaries and expectations can prevent future instances of infidelity and provide a framework for rebuilding trust.

4. Fostering Emotional Intimacy:

- Emotional Reconnection: Rebuilding emotional intimacy involves making efforts to reconnect on an emotional level, such as spending quality time together, sharing experiences, and engaging in meaningful conversations.

- Forgiveness and Healing: Forgiveness is a crucial step in the healing process. While it may take time, working towards forgiveness can help both partners move past the hurt and rebuild their emotional connection.

5. Focusing on the Future:

- Setting Goals: Setting shared goals for the future can help couples focus on rebuilding their relationship and creating a positive path forward.

- Celebrating Progress: Acknowledging and celebrating small steps towards healing and rebuilding the relationship can provide motivation and reinforce the commitment to move forward together.

Deciding to Move On:

In some cases, despite the efforts to rebuild trust and intimacy, couples may decide that separation is the best option. Recognizing when it is time to move on is important for both partners' well-being.

1. Assessing the Relationship:

- Evaluating Compatibility: Assessing the compatibility and underlying issues in the relationship can help determine whether it is worth continuing the efforts to rebuild.

- Understanding Limits: Recognizing personal limits and the extent of emotional damage can help individuals make informed decisions about staying or leaving the relationship.

2. Ending with Dignity:

- Respectful Separation: If separation is the chosen path, ending the relationship with respect and dignity can help both partners move forward with less animosity and more emotional closure.

- Seeking Support: Seeking support from friends, family, or professionals can provide emotional assistance during the process of separation and help individuals navigate the transition.

Conclusion

Infidelity is a significant challenge that can deeply impact attraction, trust, and the overall dynamics of a relationship. Understanding the different forms and motivations behind infidelity, as well as its effects on individuals and relationships, is crucial for addressing its impact.

While the road to recovery after infidelity is difficult, it is possible for couples to rebuild trust and intimacy with commitment, open communication, and professional support. Recognizing when to move on is also an important aspect of coping with infidelity, ensuring that both partners prioritize their emotional well-being.

As we continue to explore the complexities of attraction and relationships, acknowledging the challenges posed by infidelity and developing strategies to address them can empower individuals to build healthier and more resilient connections. This understanding ultimately enhances our ability to navigate the complexities of romantic relationships, fostering deeper emotional connections and overall happiness.

CHAPTER 10

THE FUTURE OF ATTRACTION

Technological Advancements and Their Impact on Relationships

The landscape of romantic relationships is continuously evolving, influenced by cultural shifts, societal changes, and, significantly, technological advancements. Technology has transformed how people meet, interact, and maintain relationships, introducing new dynamics and challenges. This chapter explores the impact of technological advancements on attraction and relationships, examining the benefits and potential pitfalls, and offering insights into navigating the digital age of romance.

The Rise of Online Dating

One of the most significant technological advancements in the realm of romantic relationships is the advent of online dating platforms. These platforms have revolutionized the way people meet and form connections.

Benefits of Online Dating:

1. Increased Accessibility:

- Broadening Horizons: Online dating platforms provide access to a larger pool of potential partners beyond one's immediate social circle, increasing the likelihood of finding a compatible match.

- Convenience: The convenience of online dating allows individuals to connect with potential partners at any time and from anywhere, fitting seamlessly into busy lifestyles.

2. Diverse Options:

- Niche Platforms: Specialized dating sites cater to specific interests, lifestyles, and demographics, helping individuals find partners who share similar values and preferences.

- Inclusivity: Online dating platforms offer a space for diverse groups, including LGBTQ+ individuals, to connect and find relationships in a more inclusive environment.

3. Efficiency:

- Algorithmic Matching: Many dating platforms use algorithms to match individuals based on compatibility factors such as interests, values, and personality traits, increasing the chances of forming successful relationships.

- Time-Saving: The ability to filter potential matches based on specific criteria saves time and allows individuals to focus on compatible partners.

Challenges of Online Dating:

1. Superficiality:

- Emphasis on Appearance: The visual nature of online dating profiles can lead to an overemphasis on physical appearance, potentially overshadowing deeper compatibility factors.

- Shallow Interactions: The ease of swiping and quick judgments can result in shallow interactions, where individuals may not invest the necessary time to get to know each other.

2. Misrepresentation:

- Profile Inaccuracies: Individuals may misrepresent themselves on their profiles, leading to disappointment and mistrust when meeting in person.

- Catfishing: Deceptive practices such as catfishing, where individuals create fake profiles to deceive others, pose risks to online daters.

3. Overwhelming Choices:

- Choice Overload: The abundance of options on dating platforms can lead to choice overload, making it difficult to commit to one person and potentially leading to indecision and dissatisfaction.

- Burnout: The repetitive nature of online dating and frequent rejections can lead to emotional exhaustion and burnout.

Social Media and Relationships

Social media platforms have become integral to modern communication, influencing how people express attraction, maintain relationships, and manage their social lives.

Impact of Social Media on Relationships:

1. Communication:

- Constant Connectivity: Social media allows for constant communication between partners, helping to maintain connection and intimacy, especially in long-distance relationships.

- Public Declarations: Public displays of affection and relationship milestones on social media can reinforce commitment and signal relationship status to others.

2. Relationship Management:

- Conflict Resolution: Social media can provide a platform for resolving conflicts through messaging and video calls, offering opportunities for immediate communication.

- Support Networks: Social media facilitates connections with friends and family, providing emotional support and advice for relationship challenges.

Challenges of Social Media:

1. Privacy Issues:

- Lack of Privacy: The public nature of social media can lead to a lack of privacy, with relationship details being visible to a wide audience.

- Boundary Violations: Partners may have differing views on what should be shared publicly, leading to conflicts over privacy boundaries.

2. Comparison and Jealousy:

- Social Comparison: Seeing curated and idealized representations of other relationships on social media can lead to unrealistic expectations and dissatisfaction with one's own relationship.

- Jealousy: Monitoring a partner's interactions with others on social media can foster jealousy and insecurity, potentially leading to trust issues.

3. Distraction:

- Reduced Quality Time: Excessive use of social media can distract from face-to-face interactions, reducing the quality time spent with a partner and affecting relationship intimacy.

Virtual Reality and Augmented Reality

Emerging technologies such as virtual reality (VR) and augmented reality (AR) are poised to further transform the landscape of romantic relationships, offering new ways to experience attraction and intimacy.

Applications of VR and AR in Relationships:

1. Virtual Dating:

- Immersive Experiences: VR can create immersive dating experiences, allowing individuals to engage in virtual dates that feel more lifelike and interactive than traditional online interactions.

- Safe Environment: VR dating provides a safe and controlled environment for individuals to get to know each other before meeting in person.

2. Long-Distance Relationships:

- Enhanced Connection: VR and AR can help bridge the physical distance in long-distance relationships by enabling shared virtual experiences and activities.

- Virtual Intimacy: These technologies can facilitate virtual intimacy, allowing couples to express affection and maintain closeness despite being geographically separated.

3. Therapeutic Uses:

- Couples Therapy: VR can be used in couples therapy to create simulated scenarios for practicing communication and conflict resolution skills.

- Exposure Therapy: For individuals with social anxiety or trauma related to relationships, VR can provide exposure therapy in a controlled and gradual manner.

Challenges of VR and AR:

1. Accessibility:

- Cost and Availability: The cost and availability of VR and AR technology may limit access for some individuals, creating disparities in who can benefit from these advancements.

- Technical Issues: Technical issues such as connectivity problems and hardware limitations can hinder the seamless use of VR and AR in relationships.

2. Authenticity:

- Virtual vs. Real: The immersive nature of VR and AR may blur the lines between virtual and real experiences, raising questions about the authenticity of virtual interactions and their impact on real-life relationships.

- Emotional Disconnect: Despite the immersive experience, VR and AR may not fully replicate the emotional depth and complexity of face-to-face interactions.

Artificial Intelligence and Relationship Algorithms

Artificial intelligence (AI) and advanced algorithms are increasingly being integrated into dating platforms and relationship management tools, offering personalized experiences and insights.

Benefits of AI in Relationships:

1. Personalized Matching:

- Enhanced Compatibility: AI algorithms can analyze vast amounts of data to identify compatibility factors and match individuals with highly compatible partners.

- Behavioral Insights: AI can provide insights into behavioral patterns and preferences, helping individuals understand their relationship tendencies and make informed decisions.

2. Relationship Coaching:

- Real-Time Advice: AI-powered relationship coaching tools can offer real-time advice and support, helping couples navigate conflicts and improve communication.

- Predictive Analysis: AI can predict potential relationship challenges based on patterns and provide proactive recommendations to address them.

Challenges of AI in Relationships:

1. Data Privacy:

- Privacy Concerns: The use of AI in relationships involves collecting and analyzing personal data, raising concerns about privacy and data security.

- Consent and Transparency: Ensuring that users understand and consent to how their data is being used is crucial for maintaining trust in AI-powered relationship tools.

2. Over-Reliance on Technology:

- Dependency: Over-reliance on AI for relationship decisions and advice can reduce individuals' autonomy and critical thinking in managing their relationships.

- Algorithmic Bias: AI algorithms may inadvertently reinforce biases and stereotypes, affecting the fairness and inclusivity of matching and relationship advice.

Navigating the Digital Age of Relationships

As technology continues to evolve, individuals and couples must navigate the benefits and challenges it brings to romantic relationships. Balancing technology use with real-life interactions and maintaining healthy boundaries is essential for fostering meaningful connections.

Strategies for Healthy Technology Use in Relationships:

1. Setting Boundaries:

- Digital Detox: Regularly taking breaks from digital devices and social media can help couples focus on face-to-face interactions and strengthen their emotional connection.

- Technology-Free Zones: Establishing technology-free zones or times, such as during meals or date nights, can enhance quality time and intimacy.

2. Communication:

- Open Dialogue: Discussing preferences and boundaries regarding technology use with a partner can prevent misunderstandings and conflicts.

- Shared Agreements: Creating shared agreements about social media sharing, online interactions, and digital communication can help maintain mutual respect and trust.

3. Mindful Engagement:

- Quality Over Quantity: Prioritizing meaningful digital interactions over frequent but superficial communication can enhance relationship satisfaction.

- Intentional Use: Using technology intentionally to support and enhance the relationship, such as through shared activities or learning opportunities, can foster a positive impact.

Conclusion

Technological advancements have significantly transformed the landscape of attraction and romantic relationships, offering new opportunities and challenges. From online dating and social media to emerging technologies like VR, AR, and AI, the digital age provides innovative ways to connect and maintain relationships.

Navigating the complexities of technology in relationships requires awareness, communication, and intentionality. By understanding the benefits and potential pitfalls of technological advancements, individuals and couples can leverage these tools to enhance their romantic connections while maintaining the authenticity and depth of real-life interactions.

As we look to the future of attraction and relationships, embracing the potential of technology while prioritizing emotional intimacy, trust, and mutual respect will be key to building resilient and fulfilling partnerships in the digital age.

CHANGING SOCIETAL NORMS AND THEIR INFLUENCES ON ATTRACTION

Changing Societal Norms and Their Influence on Attraction

Societal norms regarding attraction and relationships are continually evolving, influenced by cultural shifts, social movements, and changes in public attitudes. These changes impact how individuals perceive attractiveness, form relationships, and navigate romantic dynamics. This chapter explores the influence of changing societal norms on attraction, examining the factors driving these changes and their implications for future relationships.

Evolution of Societal Norms

Societal norms regarding attraction and relationships have undergone significant transformations over time. These changes reflect broader cultural, economic, and political developments that shape social attitudes and behaviors.

Historical Perspectives:

1. Traditional Norms:

   - Gender Roles: Historically, traditional gender roles prescribed specific behaviors and traits for men and women in romantic contexts. Men were often expected to be providers and protectors, while women were encouraged to be nurturing and supportive.

   - Marriage and Family: Traditional norms emphasized marriage and family as central to social stability and personal fulfillment. Romantic attraction was often linked to the roles individuals would play within the family unit.

2. Modern Shifts:

   - Individualism: The rise of individualism in the 20th century shifted focus towards personal fulfillment and self-expression. This change influenced romantic attraction, with greater emphasis on individual compatibility and personal growth within relationships.

- Sexual Revolution: The sexual revolution of the 1960s and 1970s challenged traditional norms regarding sexuality and relationships, promoting greater sexual freedom and the acceptance of diverse relationship structures.

Drivers of Changing Norms

Several factors drive the ongoing evolution of societal norms related to attraction and relationships. Understanding these drivers helps contextualize the changes and their impact on romantic dynamics.

Cultural Influences:

1. Media and Pop Culture:

- Representation: Media and popular culture play a significant role in shaping societal norms by depicting diverse relationship models and challenging traditional stereotypes. Representation of various relationship dynamics, sexual orientations, and gender identities fosters greater acceptance and inclusivity.

- Celebrity Influence: Celebrities and influencers often challenge conventional norms and set new trends in relationships, impacting public attitudes and behaviors.

2. Globalization:

- Cultural Exchange: Increased global interconnectedness facilitates cultural exchange, blending different norms and practices related to attraction and relationships. This exchange promotes the adoption of diverse perspectives and challenges ethnocentric views.

Social Movements:

1. Feminism:

- Gender Equality: Feminist movements advocate for gender equality and challenge traditional gender roles in relationships. These efforts promote egalitarian partnerships based on mutual respect and shared responsibilities.

- Body Positivity: Feminism also supports body positivity and challenges narrow beauty standards, encouraging a broader acceptance of diverse body types and appearances.

2. LGBTQ+ Rights:

- Acceptance of Diverse Sexualities: The LGBTQ+ rights movement has significantly impacted societal norms by promoting acceptance of diverse sexual orientations and relationship structures. This movement challenges heteronormative standards and advocates for equal rights and representation.

- Visibility and Representation: Increased visibility and representation of LGBTQ+ individuals in media and public life contribute to changing attitudes and greater acceptance of diverse relationships.

Economic and Technological Changes:

1. Work and Education:

- Economic Independence: Greater economic independence for women and increased participation in higher education and the workforce have shifted relationship dynamics. These changes promote partnerships based on equality and shared interests.

- Dual-Career Couples: The rise of dual-career couples necessitates new norms regarding work-life balance, household responsibilities, and relationship roles.

2. Technological Advancements:

- Online Dating: The proliferation of online dating platforms has transformed how people meet and form romantic connections, challenging traditional courtship norms and expanding opportunities for diverse relationships.

- Social Media: Social media influences relationship dynamics by providing platforms for connection, communication, and public displays of affection, as well as fostering new norms around digital intimacy.

Implications of Changing Norms on Attraction

The evolution of societal norms has profound implications for how individuals experience attraction, form relationships, and navigate romantic dynamics. These changes reflect broader shifts in values and priorities.

Expanding Definitions of Attractiveness:

1. Diverse Beauty Standards:

- Inclusivity: Changing norms promote inclusivity by challenging narrow beauty standards and embracing diverse body types, ethnicities, and gender expressions. This inclusivity broadens the definition of attractiveness and reduces societal pressure to conform to idealized standards.

- Authenticity: Authenticity and individuality are increasingly valued over conformity to traditional beauty norms. Individuals are encouraged to embrace their unique traits and personalities, enhancing their attractiveness.

2. Body Positivity Movement:

- Self-Acceptance: The body positivity movement promotes self-acceptance and challenges the stigmatization of different body types. This movement fosters a healthier relationship with one's body and enhances self-esteem, positively impacting romantic attraction.

- Media Representation: Increased representation of diverse bodies in media and advertising supports the body positivity movement and encourages acceptance of different forms of beauty.

Evolving Relationship Models:

1. Non-Traditional Relationships:

- Polyamory and Open Relationships: Greater acceptance of non-traditional relationship models, such as polyamory and open relationships, reflects changing norms around monogamy and exclusivity. These models emphasize consensual and ethical exploration of multiple romantic connections.

- Singlehood and Solo Polyamory: Singlehood and solo polyamory are increasingly recognized as valid relationship choices. These models prioritize individual autonomy and personal fulfillment over traditional partnership norms.

2. Gender Roles and Equality:

- Egalitarian Partnerships: Evolving norms support egalitarian partnerships where responsibilities and decision-making are shared equally. This shift challenges traditional gender roles and promotes mutual respect and collaboration.

- Shared Parenting: Shared parenting responsibilities and co-parenting arrangements reflect changing norms around family structures and gender roles, promoting balanced involvement in child-rearing.

Impact on Relationship Dynamics:

1. Communication and Emotional Intimacy:

- Open Communication: Changing norms emphasize the importance of open communication and emotional intimacy in relationships. Partners are encouraged to express their feelings, needs, and boundaries openly, fostering trust and connection.

- Emotional Intelligence: Greater focus on emotional intelligence and empathy enhances relationship dynamics, promoting understanding and support between partners.

2. Commitment and Flexibility:

- Flexible Commitment Models: Evolving norms support flexible commitment models that prioritize individual growth and adaptability. These models recognize that relationships may evolve over time and require adjustments to meet changing needs and circumstances.

- Commitment to Growth: Partners are encouraged to commit to personal and relational growth, fostering resilience and adaptability in the face of challenges.

Navigating Changing Norms in Relationships

As societal norms continue to evolve, individuals and couples must navigate these changes thoughtfully and intentionally. Embracing new norms while maintaining core values and principles is key to building healthy and fulfilling relationships.

Strategies for Navigating Changing Norms:

1. Self-Reflection and Awareness:

- Understanding Personal Values: Reflecting on personal values and beliefs helps individuals navigate changing norms and make informed decisions about attraction and relationships.

- Adapting to Change: Being open to adapting and evolving in response to changing norms can enhance relationship satisfaction and resilience.

2. Open and Honest Communication:

- Discussing Expectations: Openly discussing expectations and boundaries with partners ensures alignment and mutual understanding in navigating changing norms.

- Addressing Differences: Addressing differences in values or beliefs with empathy and respect promotes constructive dialogue and resolution.

3. Seeking Support and Education:

- Relationship Education: Engaging in relationship education and counseling can provide valuable insights and tools for navigating evolving norms and relationship dynamics.

- Support Networks: Building support networks with friends, family, and communities who share similar values and experiences can offer guidance and encouragement.

4. Embracing Diversity and Inclusivity:

- Respecting Differences: Embracing diversity and inclusivity in relationships involves respecting differences and appreciating the unique qualities each individual brings to the partnership.

- Challenging Stereotypes: Actively challenging stereotypes and biases promotes a more inclusive and accepting environment for diverse relationships.

Conclusion

Changing societal norms have a profound influence on attraction and relationships, reflecting broader cultural, social, and technological shifts. Understanding the drivers and implications of these changes helps individuals and couples navigate the evolving landscape of romantic dynamics.

As societal norms continue to evolve, embracing diversity, inclusivity, and flexibility in relationships can enhance attraction, satisfaction, and resilience. By fostering open communication, self-awareness, and mutual respect, individuals can build healthy and fulfilling relationships that adapt to changing times.

Exploring the future of attraction and relationships involves recognizing the dynamic nature of societal norms and actively engaging in the ongoing process of personal and relational growth. This understanding empowers individuals to create meaningful connections that reflect their values and aspirations, ultimately enriching their overall well-being and happiness.

PREDICTIONS FOR THE FUTURE OF LOVE AND ATTRACTION RESEARCH

The study of love and attraction has evolved significantly over the years, influenced by advances in technology, shifts in societal norms, and a deeper understanding of human behavior and relationships. As we look to the future, several emerging trends and areas of research promise to further illuminate the complexities of romantic attraction and relationships. This chapter explores predictions for the future of love and attraction research, highlighting potential developments and their implications.

Technological Integration in Relationship Research

Technology will continue to play a crucial role in advancing research on love and attraction. Innovative tools and methods will enable researchers to collect more precise data, analyze complex interactions, and gain deeper insights into romantic relationships.

Big Data and Machine Learning:

1. Large-Scale Data Analysis:

- Behavioral Insights: The use of big data will allow researchers to analyze vast amounts of information from social media, dating platforms, and other digital interactions. This analysis can reveal patterns in behavior, preferences, and relationship dynamics.

- Predictive Modeling: Machine learning algorithms can predict relationship outcomes based on behavioral data, providing insights into factors that contribute to relationship success or failure.

2. Personalized Recommendations:

- Relationship Coaching: AI-driven tools can offer personalized relationship advice and coaching based on individual behavioral patterns and preferences. These tools can help couples navigate conflicts, improve communication, and enhance intimacy.

- Matching Algorithms: Advanced matching algorithms will become more sophisticated, improving the accuracy of online dating platforms in pairing individuals with compatible partners.

Virtual Reality (VR) and Augmented Reality (AR):

1. Immersive Research Environments:

- Simulated Interactions: VR and AR can create controlled environments where researchers study romantic interactions in immersive settings. These simulations can help explore how individuals respond to different scenarios and stimuli.

- Therapeutic Applications: VR can be used in therapeutic settings to help individuals and couples practice relationship skills, such as communication and conflict resolution, in a safe and controlled environment.

2. Enhanced Long-Distance Relationships:

- Virtual Intimacy: VR and AR technologies can bridge the physical distance in long-distance relationships, allowing couples to share experiences and maintain intimacy despite being geographically separated.

Biological and Neuroscientific Advances

Understanding the biological and neurological underpinnings of love and attraction will continue to be a key focus of future research. Advances in neuroscience and genetics will provide deeper insights into the physiological processes that drive romantic behavior.

Neuroscience of Love:

1. Brain Imaging Studies:

- Emotional Processing: Functional magnetic resonance imaging (fMRI) and other brain imaging techniques will be used to study how different brain regions are involved in processing romantic emotions and attachment.

- Love and Addiction: Research will explore the parallels between romantic love and addiction, examining how similar brain pathways are activated in both experiences.

2. Neurochemical Influences:

- Hormonal Effects: Studies will investigate the role of neurochemicals such as oxytocin, dopamine, and serotonin in shaping romantic attraction and bonding. Understanding these influences can lead to new treatments for relationship-related issues.

- Stress and Love: Research will examine how stress and other external factors impact the brain's response to romantic stimuli, providing insights into the resilience of romantic relationships.

Genetics and Attraction:

1. Genetic Predispositions:

- Heritability of Traits: Future research will explore the genetic basis of traits that influence romantic attraction, such as personality characteristics, attachment styles, and sexual orientation.

- Genetic Compatibility: Studies will investigate the role of genetic compatibility in relationship success, examining how genetic similarities and differences impact attraction and long-term satisfaction.

2. Epigenetics:

- Environmental Influences: Epigenetic research will explore how environmental factors, such as early life experiences and social contexts, influence the expression of genes related to romantic behavior and attraction.

- Intergenerational Effects: Researchers will examine how epigenetic changes related to love and attachment are passed down through generations, impacting familial relationship patterns.

Psychological and Social Research

Psychological and social research will continue to deepen our understanding of the dynamics of attraction and relationships. Future studies will address emerging issues and explore new theoretical frameworks.

Emerging Theories and Models:

1. Intersectionality and Relationships:

- Complex Identities: Research will increasingly focus on how intersecting identities, such as race, gender, sexual orientation, and socioeconomic status, influence romantic attraction and relationship dynamics.

- Cultural Contexts: Studies will explore how cultural contexts shape romantic behaviors and expectations, highlighting the diversity of relationship experiences across different societies.

2. Attachment and Trauma:

- Attachment Theory: Future research will build on attachment theory, examining how early attachment experiences influence adult romantic relationships and how attachment styles can be modified through therapeutic interventions.

- Impact of Trauma: Studies will investigate the impact of trauma on romantic relationships, exploring how individuals with a history of trauma navigate attraction, trust, and intimacy.

Social and Environmental Factors:

1. Impact of Social Change:

- Digital Relationships: Research will explore how digital communication and online dating influence relationship formation and maintenance, examining the long-term effects of digital interactions on romantic satisfaction.

- Climate and Environment: Future studies will investigate how environmental factors, such as climate change and urbanization, impact romantic behavior and relationship dynamics.

2. Public Health and Relationships:

- Mental Health: Research will focus on the intersection of mental health and romantic relationships, examining how mental health issues impact attraction and relationship quality, and how romantic support can improve mental health outcomes.

- Sexual Health: Studies will continue to explore the relationship between sexual health and romantic satisfaction, addressing issues such as sexual dysfunction, consent, and safe sexual practices.

Ethical and Philosophical Considerations

As research on love and attraction advances, ethical and philosophical considerations will become increasingly important. Researchers must navigate complex questions about privacy, consent, and the impact of scientific findings on society.

Ethical Research Practices:

1. Data Privacy:

- Informed Consent: Ensuring that participants provide informed consent and understand how their data will be used is crucial for ethical research practices.

- Data Security: Protecting the privacy and security of personal data, especially in studies involving sensitive information about romantic relationships, is essential.

2. Bias and Inclusivity:

- Avoiding Bias: Researchers must be vigilant in avoiding biases in their studies, ensuring that research designs and methodologies are inclusive and representative of diverse populations.

- Inclusive Research: Promoting inclusivity in research involves addressing the unique experiences and challenges faced by marginalized and underrepresented groups.

Philosophical Implications:

1. Nature of Love:

- Defining Love: Philosophical inquiries will continue to explore the nature of love, questioning whether it can be fully understood through scientific research and how subjective experiences of love fit into empirical frameworks.

- Free Will and Determinism: Research on the biological and genetic influences on attraction raises questions about free will and determinism in romantic choices, challenging traditional notions of agency in relationships.

2. Impact on Society:

- Social Norms: The findings of love and attraction research can influence social norms and expectations, raising questions about the ethical responsibility of researchers to consider the societal impact of their work.

- Technological Mediation: The increasing role of technology in relationships prompts philosophical reflections on the authenticity of digitally mediated romantic experiences and the nature of human connection in a digital age.

Conclusion

The future of love and attraction research promises to be dynamic and multifaceted, driven by technological advancements, deeper biological and psychological insights, and evolving societal norms. As researchers continue to explore the complexities of romantic relationships, they will uncover new dimensions of attraction and provide valuable guidance for individuals and couples navigating the ever-changing landscape of love.

By embracing interdisciplinary approaches and addressing ethical and philosophical considerations, future research will enhance our understanding of the fundamental human experience of love and attraction. This knowledge will empower individuals to build healthier, more fulfilling relationships, ultimately enriching their overall well-being and happiness.

SUMMARIZING KEY FINDINGS ON THE CHEMISTRY OF ATTRACTION

The study of attraction encompasses a rich tapestry of biological, psychological, and social dimensions. This book has explored various aspects of attraction, from the role of neurotransmitters and hormones to the impact of social norms and technological advancements. As we conclude, it is essential to summarize the key findings that contribute to our understanding of the chemistry of attraction and its implications for romantic relationships.

Biological Foundations of Attraction

Neurotransmitters and Hormones:

- Dopamine: Often referred to as the "feel-good" neurotransmitter, dopamine plays a crucial role in the reward system of the brain. It is associated with feelings of pleasure and euphoria, particularly in the early stages of romantic attraction.

- Serotonin: This neurotransmitter is linked to mood regulation. During the initial phase of romantic attraction, serotonin levels can decrease, leading to obsessive thoughts about the loved one, similar to those found in individuals with obsessive-compulsive disorder.

- Oxytocin and Vasopressin: Known as the "love hormones," oxytocin and vasopressin are critical in forming emotional bonds and attachment. Oxytocin, released during physical touch and intimacy, promotes feelings of trust and bonding, while vasopressin is associated with long-term commitment and monogamy.

- Testosterone and Estrogen: These sex hormones influence sexual desire and attraction. Testosterone, present in both men and women, is linked to increased libido, while estrogen enhances sexual receptivity and fertility cues.

Genetic Factors:

- Genetic Compatibility: Research suggests that genetic factors, such as the major histocompatibility complex (MHC), play a role in attraction. Individuals tend to be attracted to partners with different MHC genes, which may enhance offspring immune system diversity.

- Heritability of Traits: Certain traits that influence attraction, such as temperament and sociability, have genetic components. Understanding these genetic influences provides insights into the heritability of romantic behaviors and preferences.

Psychological Dimensions of Attraction

Attachment Theory:

- Attachment Styles: Early attachment experiences with caregivers shape adult attachment styles, influencing romantic relationships. Secure attachment fosters healthy, stable relationships, while insecure attachment can lead to challenges such as anxiety and avoidance.

- Emotional Regulation: Attachment styles affect how individuals regulate emotions within relationships, impacting communication, conflict resolution, and intimacy.

Cognitive and Emotional Factors:

- Cognitive Biases: Cognitive biases, such as the halo effect and confirmation bias, influence perceptions of attractiveness and partner selection. These biases can lead to idealized views of potential partners and affect relationship dynamics.

- Emotional Intelligence: High emotional intelligence enhances relationship satisfaction by improving communication, empathy, and conflict resolution skills. It plays a vital role in forming and maintaining healthy romantic relationships.

Social and Cultural Influences

Social Norms:

- Gender Roles: Traditional and evolving gender roles shape expectations and behaviors in romantic relationships. While traditional roles emphasized distinct behaviors for men and women, contemporary norms increasingly support egalitarian partnerships.

- Cultural Values: Cultural values and norms influence what is considered attractive and desirable in a partner. These values vary across societies and impact relationship formation and maintenance.

Technological Advancements:

- Online Dating: The rise of online dating platforms has transformed how people meet and form romantic connections. While it offers increased accessibility and diverse options, it also presents challenges such as superficiality and choice overload.

- Social Media: Social media influences relationship dynamics by facilitating communication and public displays of affection, while also introducing challenges related to privacy, comparison, and jealousy.

Challenges and Future Directions

External Factors:

- Stress: Chronic stress impacts attraction and relationship quality by affecting emotional and physical well-being. Effective stress management and open communication are crucial for maintaining healthy relationships.

- Socioeconomic Status: Socioeconomic factors, including income, education, and occupation, influence relationship dynamics and partner selection. Addressing financial disparities and promoting economic stability can enhance relationship satisfaction.

Infidelity:

- Trust and Betrayal: Infidelity significantly impacts trust and emotional intimacy in relationships. Coping with infidelity requires open communication, professional support, and efforts to rebuild trust and emotional connection.

Future Research Directions:

- Technological Integration: Advances in technology, such as VR and AI, will continue to shape the future of attraction research, providing new tools for studying romantic behavior and enhancing relationship interventions.

- Biological and Neuroscientific Advances: Future research will delve deeper into the biological and neurological underpinnings of love and attraction, exploring genetic predispositions, neurochemical influences, and the brain's response to romantic stimuli.

- Psychological and Social Research: Emerging theories and models will address intersectionality, attachment, trauma, and the impact of social and environmental factors on romantic relationships.

Conclusion

The chemistry of attraction is a multifaceted phenomenon, influenced by an intricate interplay of biological, psychological, and social factors. Understanding these dimensions provides valuable insights into the nature of romantic relationships and the factors that contribute to their success and challenges.

As we move forward, embracing interdisciplinary approaches and addressing ethical considerations will be crucial for advancing research on love and attraction. By integrating knowledge from various fields and leveraging technological advancements, we can enhance our understanding of romantic relationships and develop effective strategies for fostering healthy, fulfilling connections.

Ultimately, the study of attraction enriches our ability to navigate the complexities of love and relationships, empowering individuals to build meaningful connections that enhance their overall well-being and happiness. As we continue to explore the dynamics of attraction, we remain committed to unraveling the mysteries of the human heart and fostering a deeper appreciation for the profound experience of love.

REFLECTIONS ON THE INTERDISCIPLINARY NATURE OF ATTRACTION RESEARCH

The study of attraction and romantic relationships is inherently interdisciplinary, drawing from a wide array of fields including biology, psychology, sociology, anthropology, and technology. This integrative approach allows for a comprehensive understanding of the complex factors that drive human attraction and shape romantic relationships. In this concluding chapter, we reflect on the interdisciplinary nature of attraction research, highlighting the key contributions from various disciplines and emphasizing the importance of continued collaboration and integration.

Biological Contributions

Neuroscience and Chemistry:

- Neurotransmitters and Hormones: Neuroscience has illuminated the role of neurotransmitters such as dopamine, serotonin, and oxytocin in romantic attraction and bonding. These chemicals influence feelings of pleasure, attachment, and trust, providing a biological foundation for understanding romantic behavior.

- Brain Imaging: Advanced brain imaging techniques, such as fMRI, have allowed researchers to observe the brain's response to romantic stimuli, revealing the neural circuits involved in love and attachment.

Genetics and Evolutionary Biology:

- Genetic Influences: Research in genetics has identified the heritability of traits related to attraction and the role of genetic compatibility in mate selection. These findings underscore the biological underpinnings of romantic preferences and behaviors.

- Evolutionary Perspectives: Evolutionary biology offers insights into the adaptive functions of attraction and mating behaviors, explaining how certain traits and behaviors have evolved to enhance reproductive success and survival.

Psychological Contributions

Cognitive and Emotional Processes:

- Cognitive Biases: Psychological research has highlighted the influence of cognitive biases, such as the halo effect and confirmation bias, on perceptions of attractiveness and partner selection. Understanding these biases helps explain why individuals are drawn to certain partners.

- Emotional Intelligence: The concept of emotional intelligence has been pivotal in explaining how individuals manage emotions, communicate effectively, and build intimate connections, all of which are crucial for successful romantic relationships.

Attachment Theory:

- Attachment Styles: Attachment theory has provided a framework for understanding how early relationships with caregivers influence adult romantic relationships. Secure, anxious, and avoidant attachment styles shape how individuals approach intimacy, trust, and dependence in their romantic lives.

Sociological Contributions

Social Norms and Cultural Contexts:

- Cultural Diversity: Sociology emphasizes the importance of cultural norms and values in shaping romantic attraction. Different societies have distinct standards of beauty, gender roles, and relationship expectations, highlighting the variability of romantic experiences across cultures.

- Changing Norms: Sociological research tracks how societal changes, such as the sexual revolution, feminist movements, and shifts in gender roles, impact romantic relationships and redefine attraction.

Social Structures and Inequality:

- Socioeconomic Factors: Sociologists examine how socioeconomic status influences romantic relationships, affecting partner selection, relationship dynamics, and stability. Economic disparities can create power imbalances and stress within relationships.

- Intersectionality: The concept of intersectionality explores how overlapping social identities, such as race, gender, and sexuality, impact romantic attraction and relationship experiences, highlighting the complexity of social influences on love.

Technological Contributions

Online Dating and Social Media:

- Digital Platforms: The rise of online dating platforms has transformed how people meet and form romantic connections. Technological advancements facilitate access to a broader pool of potential partners but also introduce challenges such as choice overload and superficiality.

- Social Media Influence: Social media shapes how individuals express attraction, maintain relationships, and manage public displays of affection. It also affects privacy, comparison, and jealousy within romantic partnerships.

Emerging Technologies:

- Virtual Reality (VR) and Augmented Reality (AR): VR and AR technologies offer new ways to experience attraction and intimacy, particularly in long-distance relationships. These technologies can create immersive dating experiences and enhance emotional connection despite physical separation.

- Artificial Intelligence (AI): AI-driven tools and algorithms improve matching accuracy on dating platforms and offer personalized relationship advice, enhancing the overall experience of forming and maintaining romantic relationships.

Integrative Approaches

Interdisciplinary Collaboration:

- Holistic Understanding: The interdisciplinary nature of attraction research underscores the need for collaboration across various fields. Combining insights from biology, psychology, sociology, and technology provides a holistic understanding of attraction and relationships.

- Comprehensive Interventions: Interdisciplinary research informs the development of comprehensive interventions and strategies to enhance relationship satisfaction and address challenges such as infidelity, stress, and mental health issues.

Future Directions:

-      Innovative   Methodologies: Continued advancements in research methodologies, such as big data analysis, machine learning, and brain imaging, will further our understanding of the complex dynamics of attraction and relationships.

- Ethical Considerations: Interdisciplinary research must also address ethical considerations, such as privacy, consent, and the societal impact of scientific findings, ensuring that research practices are responsible and inclusive.

Conclusion

The interdisciplinary nature of attraction research enriches our understanding of one of the most fundamental aspects of human life: love and relationships. By integrating knowledge from diverse fields, researchers can explore the multifaceted nature of attraction, uncovering the biological, psychological, social, and technological factors that shape romantic experiences.

As we move forward, continued collaboration and integration across disciplines will be essential for advancing the study of attraction and developing effective interventions to enhance relationship satisfaction and well-being. Embracing interdisciplinary approaches not only deepens our understanding of attraction but also empowers individuals to build meaningful, fulfilling connections that enhance their overall happiness and quality of life.

In reflecting on the insights gained from this comprehensive exploration of attraction, we are reminded of the profound complexity and beauty of human relationships. The journey of understanding attraction is ongoing, and as research progresses, we can look forward to new discoveries that will continue to illuminate the mysteries of love and deepen our appreciation for the intricate dance of human connection.

IMPLICATIONS FOR INDIVIDUALS, RELATIONSHIPS, AND SOCIETY

The comprehensive exploration of the chemistry of attraction and its multifaceted nature has significant implications for individuals, relationships, and society at large. By understanding the intricate interplay of biological, psychological, social, and technological factors, we can better navigate the complexities of romantic relationships and foster healthier, more fulfilling connections. This chapter synthesizes the key insights from our study and outlines the practical implications for individuals, relationships, and society.

Implications for Individuals

Self-Awareness and Personal Growth:

- Understanding Attraction: Gaining insight into the biological and psychological underpinnings of attraction helps individuals understand their romantic preferences and behaviors. This self-awareness can lead to more informed and intentional choices in partner selection and relationship dynamics.

- Emotional Intelligence: Enhancing emotional intelligence by developing skills such as empathy, communication, and emotional regulation can improve relationship satisfaction and resilience. Individuals who are emotionally intelligent are better equipped to navigate the ups and downs of romantic relationships.

Mental and Physical Health:

- Impact of Stress: Recognizing the impact of stress on attraction and relationships underscores the importance of managing stress through healthy coping mechanisms, such as mindfulness, exercise, and seeking social support. Addressing stress can improve both mental and physical health, enhancing overall well-being.

- Self-Esteem and Body Positivity: Embracing diverse standards of beauty and practicing self-acceptance can boost self-esteem and body positivity. Individuals who feel confident and comfortable in their own skin are more likely to form satisfying and authentic romantic connections.

Navigating Technological Advancements:

- Online Dating: Understanding the benefits and challenges of online dating can help individuals use these platforms more effectively. By being mindful of potential pitfalls such as superficiality and choice overload, individuals can approach online dating with realistic expectations and a focus on meaningful connections.

- Digital Boundaries: Establishing healthy digital boundaries, such as limiting social media use and prioritizing face-to-face interactions, can enhance relationship quality and prevent issues related to privacy, comparison, and jealousy.

Implications for Relationships

Building Healthy Relationships:

- Communication and Trust: Effective communication and trust-building are foundational to healthy relationships. Couples who prioritize open dialogue, active listening, and mutual respect can navigate conflicts more constructively and maintain emotional intimacy.

- Attachment Styles: Understanding attachment styles and their influence on relationship dynamics can help couples address insecurities and develop healthier patterns of interaction. Couples therapy and relationship education can provide tools for improving attachment security.

Coping with Challenges:

- Infidelity: Addressing infidelity requires a commitment to rebuilding trust and emotional connection. Seeking professional support and engaging in honest conversations about the underlying issues can help couples navigate the aftermath of betrayal.

- Socioeconomic Factors: Recognizing the impact of socioeconomic factors on relationships can help couples address financial stress and power imbalances. Collaborative financial planning and seeking external support when needed can enhance relationship stability and satisfaction.

Embracing Diversity and Inclusivity:

- Non-Traditional Relationships: Greater acceptance of non-traditional relationship models, such as polyamory and open relationships, reflects evolving societal norms. Couples in non-traditional relationships can benefit from open communication, clear boundaries, and mutual consent.

- Intersectionality: Understanding the role of intersecting identities in romantic relationships fosters inclusivity and empathy. Couples who respect and appreciate their diverse backgrounds and experiences can build stronger and more resilient connections.

Implications for Society

Shaping Social Norms:

- Challenging Stereotypes: Promoting diverse representations of attraction and relationships in media and popular culture can challenge harmful stereotypes and narrow beauty standards. Society benefits from a broader acceptance of different body types, ethnicities, and gender expressions.

- Gender Equality: Supporting gender equality in relationships through policies and social initiatives can promote egalitarian partnerships and shared responsibilities. Gender equality enhances relationship satisfaction and contributes to overall social well-being.

Supporting Mental Health:

- Public Health Initiatives: Integrating mental health support into public health initiatives can address the psychological aspects of attraction and relationships. Access to mental health resources, such as counseling and support groups, can improve individual and relational well-being.

- Educational Programs: Implementing educational programs that focus on emotional intelligence, relationship skills, and healthy coping mechanisms can equip individuals with the tools needed to build and maintain fulfilling relationships.

Leveraging Technological Advancements:

- Ethical Use of Technology: Ensuring the ethical use of technology in relationships involves protecting privacy, promoting informed consent, and addressing algorithmic biases. Technology companies and policymakers must work together to create a digital environment that supports healthy relationships.

- Innovation in Research: Continued innovation in research methodologies, such as big data analysis and virtual reality, can advance our understanding of attraction and relationships. Interdisciplinary collaboration and ethical considerations will be essential for meaningful progress.

Conclusion

The interdisciplinary study of attraction and relationships reveals the intricate and dynamic nature of human connection. By integrating insights from biology, psychology, sociology, and technology, we gain a comprehensive understanding of the factors that shape romantic attraction and influence relationship dynamics.

For individuals, this knowledge fosters self-awareness, emotional intelligence, and healthier relationship practices. For couples, it provides tools for building strong, resilient partnerships and navigating challenges with empathy and understanding. For society, it highlights the importance of inclusivity, mental health support, and ethical use of technology in promoting overall well-being.

As we continue to explore the complexities of attraction and relationships, it is crucial to embrace a holistic approach that considers the diverse experiences and needs of individuals and couples. By doing so, we can create a more inclusive, supportive, and understanding society that values the profound and transformative power of love.

Ultimately, the study of attraction and relationships enriches our lives by deepening our appreciation for the connections that bring us joy, fulfillment, and meaning. As we move forward, let us continue to celebrate the beauty of human connection and strive to build a world where love and attraction can flourish in all their forms.

APPENDIX

PRACTICAL APPLICATIONS

Tips for Enhancing Attraction and Maintaining Healthy Relationships

Understanding the science behind attraction and relationships can help individuals and couples improve their romantic connections. Here are some practical tips for enhancing attraction and maintaining healthy relationships:

Enhancing Attraction:

1. Self-Care and Confidence:

- Physical Health: Regular exercise, a balanced diet, and adequate sleep contribute to overall well-being and enhance physical attractiveness.

- Grooming and Appearance: Taking care of personal hygiene and grooming can boost self-confidence and make a positive impression on potential partners.

- Self-Esteem: Building self-esteem through self-acceptance and positive self-talk can increase confidence and attractiveness.

2. Emotional Intelligence:

- Empathy: Practice empathy by actively listening to your partner and validating their feelings. Understanding and sharing emotions strengthen emotional bonds.

- Communication: Open and honest communication about feelings, needs, and boundaries fosters trust and intimacy.

3. Shared Interests and Activities:

- Common Hobbies: Engaging in activities and hobbies that you both enjoy can enhance your connection and provide opportunities for quality time together.

- New Experiences: Trying new activities together can keep the relationship exciting and foster a sense of adventure and discovery.

4. Positivity and Humor:

- Positive Attitude: Maintaining a positive outlook and focusing on the good aspects of your relationship can enhance attraction and satisfaction.

- Sense of Humor: Sharing laughter and humor can strengthen your bond and create joyful memories.

Maintaining Healthy Relationships:

1. Trust and Honesty:

- Transparency: Be open and honest with your partner about your thoughts, feelings, and actions. Transparency builds trust and prevents misunderstandings.

- Reliability: Consistently keeping promises and being reliable in your actions reinforces trust and dependability.

2. Conflict Resolution:

- Effective Communication: Address conflicts calmly and respectfully. Focus on finding solutions rather than assigning blame.

- Compromise: Be willing to compromise and find mutually acceptable solutions to disagreements.

3. Emotional Support:

- Active Listening: Provide a supportive ear when your partner needs to talk. Show empathy and understanding without immediately offering solutions.

- Affection: Regularly express love and appreciation through words and actions. Physical affection, such as hugs and kisses, strengthens emotional bonds.

4. Independence and Space:

- Personal Growth: Encourage each other's personal growth and individual interests. Supporting each other's independence can strengthen the relationship.

- Respecting Boundaries: Respect your partner's need for personal space and time alone. Healthy boundaries contribute to overall relationship health.

5. Shared Goals and Values:

- Alignment: Discuss and align on key values and life goals. Shared values and goals create a strong foundation for a long-term relationship.

- Support and Encouragement: Encourage each other's aspirations and support each other's endeavors. Celebrate successes and provide comfort during challenges.

Recommended Further Reading and Resources

For those interested in deepening their understanding of attraction and relationships, the following books and resources are recommended:

Books:

1. "The Five Love Languages: The Secret to Love that Lasts" by Gary Chapman

- This book explores the concept of love languages and how understanding and expressing love in your partner's preferred language can enhance relationship satisfaction.

2. "Attached: The New Science of Adult Attachment and How It Can Help You Find—and Keep—Love" by Amir Levine and Rachel Heller

- This book provides insights into attachment theory and how understanding your attachment style can improve your romantic relationships.

3. "Hold Me Tight: Seven Conversations for a Lifetime of Love" by Dr. Sue Johnson

- Based on Emotionally Focused Therapy (EFT), this book offers practical advice for strengthening emotional bonds and fostering intimacy.

4. "The Seven Principles for Making Marriage Work: A Practical Guide from the Country's Foremost Relationship Expert" by John M. Gottman and Nan Silver

- This book outlines research-based principles for building and maintaining a healthy and fulfilling marriage.

5. "Men Are from Mars, Women Are from Venus: The Classic Guide to Understanding the Opposite Sex" by John Gray

- This classic book provides insights into gender differences in communication and emotional needs, helping couples better understand and connect with each other.

Online Resources:

1. Gottman Institute (www.gottman.com)

- The Gottman Institute offers research-based resources, workshops, and online courses for improving relationship satisfaction and communication.

2. Emotionally Focused Therapy (www.iceeft.com)

- The International Centre for Excellence in Emotionally Focused Therapy provides information and resources on EFT, a highly effective approach to couples therapy.

3. The Love Language Quiz (www.5lovelanguages.com)

- Based on Gary Chapman's "The Five Love Languages," this quiz helps individuals identify their primary love language and offers tips for improving relationship communication.

4. BetterHelp (www.betterhelp.com)

- BetterHelp offers online therapy services, including relationship counseling, with licensed therapists. This platform provides accessible support for individuals and couples.

5. TED Talks on Relationships (www.ted.com)

- TED offers a wide range of talks on relationships, love, and communication from leading experts. These talks provide valuable insights and inspiration for enhancing romantic connections.

By leveraging these tips and resources, individuals and couples can deepen their understanding of attraction and relationships, fostering healthier, more fulfilling connections.

The journey of exploring the chemistry of attraction is ongoing, and continued learning and growth will enrich our romantic lives and overall well-being.